The

Continuous

Journey of a Lifetime

::iii::

ACKNOWLEDGMENTS

I want to thank my family, my son who is my heart. And to the one who has my heart: You know who you are; Thanks for being there & listening when no one else would.

I want to thank everyone who have played a major part in my life and continue to be there. I also want to thank those who are no longer there. From the hurt and pain experienced, I have become a better woman and I truly thank you for it all.

TABLE OF CONTENTS

Acknowledgments...iv

Chapter 1: Trying to Fit In.. 1

Chapter 2: Only The Pretty Girls 5

Chapter 3: Being Rebellious Will Get You Nowhere............................ 10

Chapter 4: Biting Off More than I Could Chew 17

Chapter 5: Lights, Camera, & Drama.. 22

Chapter 6: From The Frying Pan to The Fire 30

Chapter 7: Waking Up from The Nightmare.. 35

Chapter 8: Falling in Love for The First Time 40

Chapter 9: Answering The Call.. 45

Chapter 10: Trash Day.. 49

Chapter 11: The Other Side of Lonely 59

Chapter 12: In a Great Space.. 64

Chapter 13: All For Nothing 70

Chapter 14: New Page Same Story 75

Chapter 15: Answering another Call... 80

Chapter 16: A Second Chance at Life...93

Chapter 17: Making a Move 109

Chapter 18: Spreading my Wings...112

Chapter 19: Understanding The Journey..................................119

Chapter 20: Preparing for The Transition 132

Chapter 21: Where The Journey ends with a New Beginning.............138

1

Trying to Fit In

Whoever thought August 12, a Sunday in 1973, would be the day everyone's life changed forever? I was born into this world with expectations predetermined as a birthright. I was an average sized baby, but I would take on giants from all angles. My grandfather came to the hospital that day to see me and my mother asked him to go down to the nursery to see how precious his new granddaughter was. My grandfather returned with a bewildered look on his face. My mother asked, "What's wrong?" My grandfather stated, "There must be a mix up because there is a white baby with your name on her." My mother laughed and shared, "Well I guarantee that she is the right baby since I pushed her out." My father, shared with my mother, "I think it's time to decide on a name". My mother mentioned, "We should name her Lisa". My father spoke up and said, "No because I can't say all those L's together, so we should come up with another name". My mother agreed and they both decided on Denise Nicole.

I was born into a unique family. My father was from the 7th ward and my mother was from uptown. New Orleans is known for different wards, and depending on what part of the city you were from, color played a key role.

New Orleans is divided into seventeen wards and politically, the wards are used for voting. Eventually over time the wards took on characteristics of their own. My hue was that of a high yellow shade causing my mother to want so much more for me. My mother grew up in the 3rd ward and was the middle child of my grandmother's three children. She engrossed her entire life around her education due to being the middle child. My mother experienced a lot in her life and school was her way of dealing with all the animosity that transpired around her.

After my birth, my parents stayed on New Orleans Street in the 7th ward. We remained there for a little over a year until we moved to Gentilly Woods. Gentilly Woods is a subdivision in the 9th ward of New Orleans and I had come up with a little rhyme to assist me in remembering my address. The rhyme was "5135 Metropolitan Drive" and the association was the only way I could remember where I lived.

I was a very curious child and would get into just about anything for fun because my character was strong-willed. I always wanted my way and when I could not have it, I would bang my head on the wall until I got just that. This behavior would last for months at a time and my mother didn't know what to do to stop this erratic behavior. My mother informed my grandmother that she was scared that I would really hurt myself. My grandmother informed my mother, "I have something to stop this crazy behavior and I guarantee the next time she won't do it again." My mother stated, "At this point I'm willing to try any and everything to make her stop it."

My mother had to work late one night so my grandmother agreed to watch us. By now, my sister was born so we would stay at my grandmother's house until my mother got off work. My grandmother had a crystal candy jar in her dining room and I always had my eyes on getting to it. That night my grandmother put some new candy in the jar and I had to have some. The candy was butterscotch disks and I just knew my grandmother would give me some; but when she told me "No" I had begun banging my head on the wall. While in the process of banging my head, my grandmother poured a pitcher of ice-cold water all over me. I immediately screamed and sat in the corner. I had to admit; the cold water got me together real quick, and from that moment on I never hit my head again.

I was the lightest one of the bunch and felt like the black sheep at the same time. I did whatever I could to get attention and to take away from the color of my skin. I never realized as I got older there would be more obstacles to overcome. Fitting in was hard and I never knew how to express myself in the right way. Once the freezing water put me in check I found another way to draw attention, but still in the wrong ways. I began to pick fights with my sister, and my mother couldn't understand what was wrong with me. Every time she looked up there was something new I got into.

Still trying to fit in and as I got older, I tried to make as many friends as possible, but at times I still felt awkward and I never knew why. I guess I was searching for an answer to a question to which I would never get an answer. My parents were both employed and I never wanted for anything, but to me, that still wasn't enough to make me feel good about myself.

My father was a police officer and my mother worked for the federal government and I was given all the luxuries any child could ever want. So why was I so unhappy with my life? That question would take years to answer. I knew early I was different and it was brought to my attention once I started school. Even though we lived in Gentilly; we went to school uptown since my parents worked two different schedules. My grandparents would always watch us until one of my parents would pick me up at night. My grandmother was a beautician and my grandfather was a Longshoreman so I was never exposed to the thought of "Not Having".

When I started Kindergarten, I realized the class contained an array of skin tones and I began to feel a little better. It did not answer the proverbial question which was dangling over my head, but at least it put my mind at ease. I enjoyed Kindergarten and, at times, wanted to stay at school because I felt comfortable there. I made a few friends and I was never questioned about my skin tone.

I was older now and on certain days after school when my grandparents or my parents could not pick my sister and I up from school we would go to the babysitter's house. I was in the 2nd grade and we would go to the babysitter until someone could pick us up. My sister and I would spend a lot of time there and the babysitter did all she could to make sure we were taken care of until it was time for us to leave. We enjoyed being there until one day my life changed forever. I was still confused about who I was, and the new turn of events had me questioning the reason for my existence.

2

ONLY THE PRETTY GIRLS

The babysitter lived on Dryades Street right off Louisiana Ave. The house was located uptown and not too far from my grandmother's house. My sister and I would go there at least twice a week which was fine with me. The babysitter made sure all the children she watched in the evening were well taken care of. She prepared snacks making sure we all took naps until our parents could pick us up for the evening. I enjoyed going to the babysitter because she made me feel wanted and I never felt like I needed to fit in. She lived in a shotgun house, but it was considered a camel back since the stairs were in the back of the house leading to an upstairs bedroom. Camel backs were common in New Orleans and were known for their beauty and were heavily populated in the uptown areas. I was at the babysitter for first and second grades so being there had become routine for me as if I were tying my shoes.

The babysitter, which we called Nanny, had a son and he would come over to the house from time to time. The babysitter had to leave this particular day to run an errand and asked her son to stay until she returned. She mentioned to her son we were all asleep, so he shouldn't have any problems. I got up a few minutes looking for her and her son mentioned she would be right back. He then asked me if there was anything wrong and I told him I wanted some water. At the time, her son had to be 19 years of age or maybe 20. I was only seven years old, so I looked at him as an adult and never imagined how much my life would change in a matter of a moment.

After he gave me the water to drink; he sat at the table until I finished. Once I finished the water, her son asked me to go in the front room. I told him I was supposed to go back upstairs and go to sleep. He then mentioned since he was an adult it would be fine if I would go in the front with him. Being only seven, I figured it would be alright and didn't think anything of it. I followed him into the front room and he asked me to sit on his lap. I thought it was okay and he mentioned he wanted to read me a story to help me go back to sleep. He had begun to read the story, but he also began to put his hands in my underwear. While doing it he mentioned, "This is what happens to pretty girls and it will be our little secret." He had put his fingers in my vagina and played with it for a little while until the babysitter returned.

When Nanny returned home she stated to her son, " Why was Denise up and not sleeping with the other children?" Her son mentioned that I wanted a glass of water and since I couldn't go right back to sleep he read me a story. I was no longer sitting on her son's lap, but on the sofa, so the babysitter had no idea what had taken place. Before going back upstairs her son leaned over and said, "It's our little secret and if you tell anyone they would be jealous of me. So don't tell anyone, not even my parents." When my mother came to pick us up, Nanny's son gave me a look to make sure I wouldn't say a word.

I was quiet on the way home and mother asked, "What's wrong?" I told her, "My tummy hurts, and all I wanted to do was lay down once I got home." When we got home I asked mother if I could get in the tub because that might help my tummy feel better. My grandmother always had a ritual of taking a bath with Palmolive dish detergent after having a long day at work. It was supposed to make her skin soft, so I decided it would make what happened go away. I stayed in the tub to the point my skin started to prune up. I figured I was dirty and if Palmolive got the dishes clean it would do the same for me.

I was glad the incident took place towards the end of the week and hoped I would never see the Nanny's son never again. A new week started, and we usually would go to Nanny's house on Tuesdays and Fridays. We would go on those days because my grandmother was extremely busy doing hair. Nanny's son was not there on the following Tuesday and I didn't feel scared being there. I really enjoyed being by Nanny and she made being there exciting, but her son made me so scared I didn't want to go there anymore. Since he told me it was our little secret I made sure I never said anything because I didn't know what he might do if I did. A couple of weeks had passed and I never saw Nanny's son again, so I figured I never had to worry about him anymore.

It was time to go to Nanny's house after school and it had begun to rain. Nanny hurried to fix our snacks, so we could take our naps until our parents picked us up for the evening. While I was asleep, I began to feel someone touching on me and when I opened my eyes it was her son standing over me. Since there were other children in the room he asked me to get underneath the bed. Her son would always remind me, "This is what happens to pretty girls" and since I was so pretty he couldn't help himself. While lying under the bed, he proceeded to put his fingers in my vagina and he stated, "Don't make a noise so my mom won't come up here and stop me from showing you how much I really care for you." The entire time it was happening I wanted him to stop since I was feeling extremely uncomfortable. This torture lasted for at least four months and I felt trapped because I was truly scared to say anything because I didn't think anyone would believe me.

The following week Nanny's son was arrested and spent time in jail for a drug charge. I overheard Nanny on the phone trying to figure out what she was going to do. She didn't know whether to leave him there or to get him out. I had to admit, I was happy he was in jail and with him being there the torture would stop and it did for a long time.

Time passed, and I was now in the eighth grade. I was watching the news and saw Nanny's son was arrested for rape. The very next day I was in the car with my mother, but I figured it wasn't the best time to say anything now that so much time had passed. I figured no one would believe me and I held on to the secret for a very long time. This experience had me so confused and my promiscuity was placed in the forefront at a very early age. I decided I would use this type of behavior to get the boys in my neighborhood to notice me. My mind was so messed up that I believed using my body was the right way to fit in, not knowing this was the wrong way to do it.

I was 14 years of age and I forced the boy down the street to have sex with me. It happened at his home because his parents would get home late. I was friends with his sister and I would tell my mother I was going down the street to play, but my goal was to get him to notice me instead. I internalized what was said to me, "That's what happens to pretty girls" so I would do whatever it took to accomplish that goal. I accomplished what I had set out to do, we had sex. After it was over, I was very disappointed because what I heard and what took place didn't match up. Instead, the boy down the street mentioned it to his friends and we would have sex regularly and it never got any better. I was only doing it so he would notice me, not realizing he couldn't care less. He made me seem like a slut who would have sex with anybody.

He didn't care who knew we were having sex. On one occasion, he had his friends in the closet watching the entire time. He even asked, "Could I run a train on you?" I didn't know what that meant and I told him "No".

From that moment on he stopped speaking to me. Trying to fit in back fired and I lost my virginity for nothing. When people would see me they would turn their noses up and say terrible things about me. My biggest concern was my behavior getting to my parents and I didn't need them to know. I never told them anything in my life because they had such high expectations and I knew if they found out they would be disappointed. My parents wanted so much more of me, but I could never meet their expectations.

This was when I started my road to self-destruction and felt no one understood me. I couldn't explain how I felt and knew no one else would either even if I tried to. My parents were more concerned about what they wanted for me; they never focused on the problems I was experiencing at the age of 14. My little escapade took place during the summer as I prepared for high school. All my awkward moments shot me down instead of building me up. I wanted to attend a well-renowned public high school and my mother informed me I wouldn't make it there and placed me in a Catholic school instead. I was informed that the Catholic school would give me a better opportunity to learn as well as how to interact with other ethnicities which would advance me in my future endeavors. I did not have a say in the matter and I was off to a Catholic school in the fall of '87.

3

BEING REBELLIOUS WILL
GET YOU NOWHERE

I was now starting high school. I felt my life was over because who wanted to go to a school with a bunch of girls?! To make things worse, it was Catholic too. Just the thought of it was pure torture so I made it up in my mind I would do all I could to get put out. Of course, being a child, my reasoning was vastly underdeveloped and I thought if I could get out I would be able to go to the Public School of my choice. I started my plan early in the year; I figured I would need enough time for it to build up in order to work the way I wanted it to.

Everything my parents told me not to do, I did, just to get a reaction from them. If they said go right I went left to make them mad. I figured they didn't care about me so why should I care about them. I befriended some of the girls at school, but not for the right reasons; but only to have my plan put in place so I could make my move. There was this girl named Tracey I had become extremely close with and what made it sweeter was our fathers knew each other well. Over time I would tell Tracey what I was trying to accomplish and she agreed because she didn't want to go to the school either. At least now I had someone who understood how I felt and was willing to go along with the plan.

The school year went on and my grades were not the best. My parents were angry as I knew they would be, but I really didn't care. I was grounded for weeks at a time allowing me to come up with more ways to make them angry. My father was my favorite and I really didn't want to make him angry, but it was a packaged deal. At times, I would wonder if I was adopted because my mother and I were so different. It seemed like we never got along, almost like oil and water to say the least. I often wondered if I was mixed up at birth with someone else's child especially after being told about what my grandfather said when I was born.

The closer it got to the end of my freshman year I practically lived in the principal's office, with my parents being called regularly. My father would be there pretty much all the time because he worked at the police station near the school. He would always say, "How do you expect to be anything in life acting this way?" Remember, he was my favorite so I felt bad he was going through this, but I was in too deep with my plan of getting kicked out of school. Tracey and I would cut class and would never turn our assignments in on time and always showed up late for all our classes. By the time the school year ended, Tracey and I realized we didn't accomplish what we set out to do; the only consolation was detention for an entire month. The school year had ended, causing Tracey and I to stop speaking plus I was tired of trying to get kicked out. I realized I would make the best of being in school and tried to make some new friends.

I barely made it to my sophomore year and I continued to rebel, just not in the same way.

The only person I felt I could talk to was my aunt, Shayna, since we were so close in age.

Shayna was 17 years older than me and she insisted I never put a handle on her name by calling her Aunt Shayna. When you're from the South we were always told to address an adult in the correct manner until you are told not to do so. Shayna saw I would bother her sister, so she would take me for the weekends to give my mother a break. I enjoyed spending weekends with my aunt in Algiers.

Algiers was considered a part of New Orleans, but it was across the Mississippi River.

Algiers is considered to be the second oldest neighborhood and is known as the 15th ward. It was considered to be the birthplace of jazz after many African American jazz artists lived there in the early 1900s. Algiers had very strong roots to Africa and was the arriving point and holding spot for many slaves once they came from Algeria. Also, Algeria was a sovereign state in North Africa on the Mediterranean coast and slaves were exported from Algeria before being shipped across the Mississippi River.

Now that you've gotten a history lesson, it was summer time and Shayna shared with me how my mother really felt, which made me feel even more insecure of myself. Shayna shared that my mother had considered giving me away because something must have been wrong with me. My mother could not understand why I didn't act like the other children and why I was so rebellious. Once it was said I made up my mind I was going to do whatever I wanted and didn't care who liked it.

It was fall and time for me to start a new school year. I befriended two new girls and put my focus on other things. Sophomore year started off well and I did not feel as awkward, as I did, in the first year of high school. I started dating a guy from a co-ed public high school and that made me seem normal. Everything seemed to go well, but I resorted back to what I thought would keep a guy around. Albert, in the beginning, treated me great, but that changed pretty quickly. He picked me up from school one day and brought me back to his parents' house. Albert was quiet the entire drive and I asked him "What was going on?" He immediately said "Nothing". I began to wonder what was going on in my mind. We pulled up in front of his parents' house. Albert told me, "We gone have to hurry up because my parents will be home soon." I said, "Okay" and we started having sex. Once we were done he did something I would have never imagined he would do. He said, "Hurry up and put your clothes on and get out." I was confused and asked, "How am I going to get home?"

Albert said, "That's not my problem because my new girlfriend is on her way here."

After I got kicked out I began looking for change so I could catch the bus to get home. I didn't want to call my parents because no one knew where I was. I only had enough money to get one transfer. After changing buses, I had to make up my mind quickly on what I needed to do next. When the bus had come, I gave the Bus Driver the piece of transfer I had and hoped he wouldn't pay attention. I immediately sat in a seat all the way in the back of the bus with my head down. The Bus Driver didn't pull off from the stop and caught my attention and called me to come back to the front of the bus. The Bus Driver told me to get off the bus and all I could do was get off. I started to cry because I knew I had to walk at least five miles home. I made it home and my mother asked me "What took you so long to get home. You must have been playing around?" I immediately came up with "I had to stay late because I had detention." My mother sent me to my room and yelled "You need to do better, or you will remain in the 10th grade."

I was still upset by what took place the day before that I really didn't want to talk to anyone at school. It was the third period and I was tapped on the back by Asia. Asia mentioned, "I heard that Albert kicked you out of his house yesterday." I immediately denied what was said. I told Asia "I don't know what you are talking about", and turned my head. I felt sick to my stomach and thought I was going to pass out. Asia then tapped me on my shoulder stating "The reason why I know is because Albert dumped you for me." All I could think about was who else knew about what happened. Asia and I never saw eye to eye and telling everyone she stole my boyfriend would make her feel great. The rest of the day I was praying Asia had not told anyone else about what happened. This situation really put my self-esteem in the toilet and Asia was the one who took joy in flushing.

To pull attention from the situation I tried to get the attention of whoever wanted to be with me. I figured what the hell since my reputation was probably messed up anyway I would do what I wanted. I would jump from one guy to the next because remember "This is what pretty girls do." Now I don't want you to think I slept with every guy, but who would believe me if I did or didn't. I already mentioned Tracey stopped speaking to me and now she is friends with Asia, so you already know Asia told Tracey all about what Albert had done to me.

My days of being rebellious eventually backfired on me. I met a guy who went to a Catholic school for all boys and I thought he would take my mind off the incident with Albert. His name was Jeremy and he was two years older than me. Jeremy was such a charmer and would charm the pants off a mermaid. In the beginning, he was wonderful, but after a few months he had become very possessive. Jeremy told everyone I belonged to him and if he ever found out I was with someone else then there would be a price to pay. Jeremy was considered the big man on campus so no one would take the chance when he staked his claim with me.

I was at home sick one day with the flu and was feeling horrible. Jeremy called and asked if he could come over since he knew I wasn't feeling good. When he got to the house he wasn't alone. Jeremy got his friend, Robert, to bring him to the house. Jeremy asked if his friend could come in and I told him "No" because he should not have been there in the first place. Jeremy said, "I won't be here long plus it's hot outside and he could sit in the living room." I agreed, and Jeremy's friend had come in & sat in the living room. Jeremy stated, "I know you are sick, but I just wanted you to feel good." After saying that he forced his way in and we had sex. I didn't think anything of it since we had sex a few times before. Once he was done he got up and left the room. Not knowing what he was doing; I laid back down because I really wasn't feeling good at all. I had my eyes closed and when Jeremy returned he asked a question which blew my mind. He asked, "Could my boy have some?". I looked at him as if he had fallen and bumped his head on a piece of cement. I immediately yelled "NO", and told him and his friend to get out of the house.

A few weeks had passed and people at school started looking at me strangely. I would ask what was going on and no one would tell me anything. The friends that I had at the Catholic boy's school would not speak to me anymore and the few people who did speak to me at school kept their distance. I did not know what to think and figured whatever it was it would eventually pass. I could not help but to think that the situation with Albert had spread. I thought that the incident was not that important so I just guessed that whatever it was would blow over.

A month had passed and the only two friends I had finally told me what was going on. Sam shared that her brother told her it was spreading around the school a bunch of boys had sex with me and two of them were Jeremy and his friend, Robert. I couldn't say anything because I was shocked. During the ordeal; Jeremy and I were still dating, and he never said a word to me. When I questioned him about what was said, he stated " I don't want to be associated with someone like you" and ended the relationship. He also shared it was in his best interest to end the relationship since I was crowding his space. Jeremy hung up the phone and all I could do was cry. I felt completely alone and did not have anyone to talk to. Even if I tried to talk to Shayna; I would be taking a chance of my parents finding out. The remaining portion of my 10th grade year turned out to be the worst year of my life, so I began to isolate myself from everyone.

4

BITING OFF MORE
THAN I COULD CHEW

I was happy my 11th grade year was now here; I wished it was over, just as fast, so high school could be a passing memory.

It was time for Thanksgiving, but I really didn't have much to be thankful for. I met Keith and he lived in the neighborhood. I was skeptical at first of hanging out with him since he went to the same school with Jeremy. I figured if he didn't say anything about my past, then neither would I. Over time Keith and I began dating which lasted over a year. I didn't realize then being with Keith would be the start of an abusive pattern of relationships I would experience well into the thirties. Keith was very controlling and I didn't see it for what it was worth. I thought the things Keith was doing showed how much he cared about me, but Keith would have me watch so he could know my every move. Keith's friend Henry would tell me from time to time what Keith was doing in the relationship and I refused to believe him thinking Henry wanted me instead. I was so naïve, thinking he only wanted me and I refused to believe he was also dating someone from another all girl

Catholic school. I asked Keith about Rhonda, and he pretended he didn't know what I was talking about. I let it go, never bringing it up again until I saw it for myself; Keith and Rhonda out together.

I could have approached them; instead I just walked away not speaking to Keith for a few days. I got the nerve to confront him regarding the situation; not knowing my life would make a drastic change. Keith informed me "I get whatever I want and you are one of those things." He also mentioned, "You are going to be fine with it and when I'm ready, I'll let you out of this." I didn't know what to do so I allowed the control to continue until I got tired of dealing with it.

I figured if Keith was going to have his fun I would too. Being rebellious was my way of fighting back and sometimes I would go too far. I allowed Keith to continue having the best of both worlds and playing the game the way he wanted it. Keith had come over to my parents' house and I was not feeling good at the time. We were sitting in the den playing cards and Keith leaned over and whispered in my ear, "I think it's time that we go our separate ways." I was so enraged that before I realized it, I had pinned Keith up against the wall with my arm pressed into his neck. My mother came running yelling my name saying, "Leave Keith alone." Keith left immediately and I felt better to have him gone out of my life. Surprisingly, the next day Keith apologized with three dozen roses and he stated, "I was wrong and should have not said those things to you." I sat at the table crying feeling like it was my fault entirely. Keith then said, "Let's try this again and things will be different." It sounded good, so I agreed to get back together which caused the control to escalate, not knowing I was caught up in what was called the "Honeymoon Phase". I will explain more about what the "Honeymoon Phase" is later on.

I never imagined my life would remain on a roller coaster and at this point in my life, I was ready to get off. Things between Keith and I continued to take a downward spiral. It was my last year in high school and things continued to get crazier. I was mad, as usual, with Keith so I decided to not answer his calls. My mother asked me to go to the store and I picked up some items that she needed. As I was checking out, I was approached by this guy named Joseph. He asked me, "Would it be okay to take you out to get something to eat?" He was nice looking, and I figured it was Friday so why stay at home bored. The same night Joseph picked me up from my parents' house and we went out on a date. Before leaving, Joseph met my parents and my mother even made the comment "He seems like a respectable guy."

We went to dinner and then to the movies. Joseph stated, "I really enjoyed myself and hopefully we can go out again." I agreed and thought to myself, "Finally he seems like he's not crazy and maybe I could finally leave Keith alone." After the movie, Joseph asked, "Would it be okay if we stopped by my apartment first, I need to pick up something since it is on the way to your house?" I said "Okay" and then we went to his apartment complex.

Once we got there, Joseph stated "I'll be right back, but you could come in if you wanted to." I told Joseph, "I'm fine and I'll wait out here until you come back." He remained inside for about ten minutes before coming outside stating "I'm on the phone with my mom and it may be a while." He then stated, "I don't feel comfortable with you being out here by yourself and I should only be a few more minutes." I was still kind of cautious, but I didn't feel comfortable staying outside either. I sat on the sofa waiting for Joseph to come back into the room to take me home.

Everything I thought earlier about Joseph had gone right out the window. After he had come out of the room he sat next to me and asked me "Do you need anything?" and before I knew it he had me pinned down on the sofa. I screamed, "Please get off me.", but he didn't move and began pulling off my clothes. Joseph then stated," You know you want this. You wouldn't have come in if you didn't want it, now shut up until I'm done." I felt paralyzed and was imagining I was somewhere else. I didn't move because I just wanted it over, so I could go home. All I could think about was being back in the dish washing liquid to clean myself off. Once he finished he threw my clothes at me and said, "You better not say anything because I will hurt you if you do." All I wanted to do was get out of there and I told him, "You don't have to worry." I felt so dirty and didn't want him to see me cry so I asked, "Could you bring me home?"

I was so angry and was scared at the same time. I never said anything about the ordeal and kept it to myself hoping that no one would ever find out. I started talking to Keith again and tried to have sex with him as much as possible. I was always seen as a slut and I figured why not carry myself in that manner. Why not because I was told early in life this was what happens to pretty girls, so I needed to play the part. Keith didn't understand why I was always throwing myself at him, but he didn't turn it down. We had sex pretty much everywhere because this was my way to deal with all the pain I was dealing with. In a matter of months, I had become pregnant. I didn't have any thoughts of how I felt and hid that as long as I could. I eventually told Keith and he was excited by the news. Keith's controlling ways had stopped, but I still was numb to what I was going to do with the thought of being pregnant. Even though Keith wanted to keep the baby that was something I knew I wasn't ready for.

Still stressed by the rape and now being pregnant, it all took a major toll on my life. I tried to act like nothing was going on, but my body had a completely different plan. I began feeling sick one morning and I felt extremely weak. I stayed in bed for as long as I could, but the pains in my stomach became too much to bear. I remember getting out of bed and making my way to the kitchen to tell my mother I wasn't feeling good. In the process of telling my mother, I must have passed out because all I remember was waking up at the hospital.

Once I woke up, the doctor told me, "The baby was in your tube and there was nothing I could do to save the baby." I was also told I would never be able to have any children in the future. I was still out of it, but I knew exactly what the doctor was talking about. By the time I got home my mother was furious, but she knew the only person I could have been pregnant for was Keith and she liked Keith for some strange reason. Once I started feeling better I told Keith and he got quiet. Keith then mentioned "I need to go because my mother will be home soon." I knew then I had bitten off more than I could chew. Not only did I bite off more than I could chew, I couldn't even keep it down. The devastating news put an end to the relationship I had with Keith. I was glad because I didn't think I needed the pressure of dealing with so many losses and I wasn't even eighteen yet.

Graduation day had finally come, and I hoped all the drama I experienced doing high school would finally be over or at least I thought. Right before the summer started, I met someone through a close friend and he seemed like a nice person. He was very low key, and I figured this would be the opportunity I needed being in a relationship without drama. His name was Aaron and our relationship actually went extremely well. Things were great during the summer and then the relationship shifted when he went away to college and I stayed in the city. Aaron mentioned a long-distance relationship could work, but I knew in my heart it wouldn't, so I ended it. We remained friends and agreed once college was over I could move out there and we would start the relationship again. I thought to myself every time I thought my life would go in the right direction, it always went off track and led back to more trouble.

5

LIGHTS, CAMERA, & DRAMA

I t was Fall of 1991 and I attended a well-renowned HBCU in New Orleans. Here, I figured I could start over and make the best of my college years since my high school years were truly miserable. Being the new kid on the block, no one could remind me of all the past things that had transpired in my life. Once on campus, I could breathe a breath of fresh air and I felt as if this was truly the beginning of a new journey in my life.

Still dealing with the past hurts and pains, I quickly made friends anticipating this would make things better now that I was older. I never gravitated well to females, so my first intent was to seek out some new male friends and I could accomplish this goal immediately when I had run into Henry. I knew Henry from the all boy high school and he was friends with Keith, ironically enough. I hoped he didn't mention or remember anything about dating his friend. Henry and I had become very close and he later introduced me to two other people which I had also hung with. Their names were Amberlyn and Andrew. Both Henry and Andrew were sophomores and Amberlyn was a freshman too. I had to admit, my freshman year was the best year of my life in comparison to what I went through growing up.

During my freshman year, no one looked at me as ever doing anything wrong and for once I was able to build up my self-esteem. I was doing well in school, I had a good set of friends, and Henry was like my big brother making sure no one would do anything to hurt me. Wow….did things really turn around for me! Amberlyn and I had become really close. As I mentioned earlier, I never gravitated to females, but I found myself trusting Amberlyn enough to the point we were hanging out all the time. Amberlyn was a loyal friend and I needed at this period of my life. I still had some of my destructive ways, but Amberlyn never criticized me no matter what happened. Amberlyn did voice her concerns, but she was never judgmental.

My friendships had become very strong with Henry, Andrew, and Amberlyn, but I did manage to associate with some people who were questionable. As I made it through college my grades remained extremely high. My actions, on the other hand, had begun to bottom out. I began dating a few individuals who my parents didn't approve of, and knowing this I continued to see them anyway. I really didn't have a reason for doing it but staying out of trouble had become extremely boring to me. My behaviors had become so bad I would have several guys showing up at my parents' house at all hours of the night to pick me up. My father stated, "You must stop this. You're not going to have all these boys coming to my house looking for you and I'm not breaking up any fights behind this."

I backed off some and redirected my energy now to something new. I began looking for a job and started working at a famous shoe store. I worked at the shoe store for several months and not too long after I started an affair with the store manager, Larry. The affair lasted for over a year, but I never shared it with Amberlyn because I did not want her to be disappointed in me. The questionable bunch I hung out with, they thought it was cool. The affair started with simple flirting but turned into having sex in the stock room often. The affair had become boring to me and I wanted out. I mentioned to the store manager, "I don't want to do this anymore" and he stated," You are playing by my rules and if you don't you won't have a job." So, I continued to have sex because I wanted to keep working all the hours and having the extra money whenever I needed it. I had an addiction to shoes and working made sure I could have them.

The affair continued, not by choice, until Larry was transferred to another store. I got excited thinking this was my chance to finally get out of this mess since I really did not know how it started in the first place. Before the transfer, Larry called a meeting to discuss what was about to take place. He mentioned he would be transferring, and he would be taking certain people with him. Well, of course, I was one of the individuals he chose to go with him. Once I got to the new store the affair continued and things didn't change. It got to the point I began to use school as my reason for not being able to work hoping he would get mad and want to fire me.

Over time my plan backfired, and I was given a key to open and close the store. Weeks went by, and one morning as I was opening the store and the Assistant Manager asked,

"Why are you opening and where is Larry?" I saw this as an opportunity to either get fired or get transferred out of the store because I was truly tired of this madness. I told Donnette the entire story and I already knew she didn't like me. Hopefully she would say something about the whole situation and it would come to an end. As always, the situation turned out completely different from what I anticipated. The lights were turned on and the camera was rolling, and the drama had begun.

All in a matter of days I had begun receiving phone calls that were disturbing. I was still living with my parents and all the calls were coming to my parents' phone. The calls were from Larry's wife. I told her, "If you want to have this conversation you should call my number" and she refused to listen. When my parents would answer the phone she would hang up, but when I would answer she would make several threats for me to leave her husband alone. The next day I confronted Larry and he stated, "I know about what my wife is doing because she put me out last night." He asked me, "How did she find out?" I immediately told him, "I told Donnette." He then said, "Why did you tell her?" I said, "She questioned me about why I was opening the store and why I was getting so many hours if she was supposed to be the Assistant Manager." All Larry could do was just stand there and say nothing. Larry stated, "I will pull some strings, and have you moved to another store." I was actually glad because I was truly tired of dealing with him anyway.

Eventually I told Amberlyn about the transfer to another store and Amberlyn asked "Why?" I could not tell her what happened and mentioned "I just wanted something closer to home." Amberlyn said, "That makes sense" and we changed the subject. As I was waiting for the transfer, I had more time to hang with Amberlyn hoping I could clear my head and put the situation behind me. I would spend a lot of time at Amberlyn's house because her younger sister Diana had leukemia and she would do all she could to help her mother. Amberlyn saw I was quiet which was very unusual, and she asked, "Is everything okay?" I stated,

"Sure you know school is getting rough now that we are getting closer to our junior year." Amberlyn agreed and we started working on the assignment for class and she never brought it up again.

Now the camera was rolling, long after the lights were off, the drama was turning out to be the picture I never expected. The very next week I began working at the shoe store Larry requested for me to go to. When I started working at the new store, I knew it would be trouble from the start. I was dating Andrew and we had a relatively good relationship since he did not know about the affair. I worked at the new shoe store for a few weeks and the Assistant Manager, Ted, made it his business to have me around him all the time. I was not interested in him, especially after what took place with

Larry. I just was not up for it at all and only wanted to work so I could make some money.

Ted did everything he could to get my attention. I made it plain to him that I was not interested several times, and he was not my type. I had worked at the shoe store for about a month and noticed the schedule had changed, but not to my advantage. One evening I got a copy of the schedule for the month and I took it to the store manager, Jimmy and asked, "Why am I always closing with Ted?" Jimmy stated, "He is the one who makes the schedule and if that's what he wants then that's how it will be." I left the office extremely pissed because I figured the two of them were in on it together. The first night we worked together Ted would make small talk and I would ignore him. Once the store was closed for the evening, I quickly got out of there, so I didn't have to speak to him.

Several shifts had ended, and on every shift Ted would try something different to get my attention, but nothing he did worked until he went to the far extreme. Remember I said earlier I was dating Andrew and this particular night he was supposed to pick me up from work. Once the store was completely closed I waited outside for him and Andrew never showed up. Ted made the statement, "What's wrong?" I told Ted, "I'm waiting for my boyfriend to pick me up and he should have been here by now." Ted proceeded to say," Oh he called, and I told him that you were having your mother pick you up." I was so angry I began to hit him in the chest until he grabbed my wrist. Ted stated, "I could bring you home since I'm the reason your boyfriend's not coming." I said, "I guess since I don't have a ride and I don't want my mom to get out of bed."

Ted, of course, didn't bring me straight home. He mentioned "Since I screwed up, let me get you a Daiquiri and we can sit on the lake and get to know each other." I agreed; I figured it was the least he could do since he messed everything else up. We got to the lake and he started to tell me about himself and I really wasn't impressed, but I tried to act like I was. The entire time Ted was talking, I was trying to figure out how I was going to tell Andrew what happened. Ted got up and walked to his car and got a small bag of marijuana. When he pulled the bag out, that's when I started to see him differently. I immediately asked Ted, "Do you have a dealer?" Ted asked me," What do you know about this?" I mentioned, "Don't worry about what I know and who is your supplier?" Ted said, "It could be me." I thought about it and agreed to entertain him since he could supply what I needed.

Now we both got what we wanted, I guess. Ted didn't seem to be so bad and I did not mind being around him because I definitely got what I wanted, and it was the marijuana. I had to make a decision on what to do with Andrew. We talked about where we were with our relationship and we decided we should just be friends. I only knew Ted for a few months, but I was only concerned he'd supplied my habit and the best thing about it; I did not have to pay for it. Ted also realized as long as he supplied my habit I would always be in his presence. It was quite dysfunctional, but the marijuana allowed me to escape for just a little while before having to come back to reality. I never really knew what to expect when I was with Ted though. I never wanted for anything because whatever I wanted I got it; Ted made sure of it. Over time I learned most of the things I received were stolen and Ted was a sheep in wolves' clothing. As I got deeper into my habit, expense free, Ted would make sure I stayed deeper in it, so he could keep me under his control.

It was December of 1993 and I really started feeling bad and wasn't sure what the reason could be. I thought it might be a sinus infection, so I went to the doctor for a checkup. After seeing the doctor, I was prescribed antibiotics to clear up the infection. Like clockwork I would hang out with Ted, but this particular day was different. When I got to his apartment he had my favorite alcohol which was vodka and stated, "I'm celebrating a possible new venture." I asked, "What new venture!!" Of course, I got no response. I asked the same question again and Ted stated, "Don't worry about it, just know it is very good." We continued to drink, and one thing led to the next. After we had sex, we smoked, and I just sat on the sofa until my high wore off.

It was now January of 1994, and my life made a major detour and the roller coaster ride lasted until 2008. I was in my mother's kitchen and she noticed I wasn't looking good. I told her "I woke up feeling really funny and I can't explain the feeling." My mother said, "You look a little thick in the hips…. Are you pregnant?" I told her I don't think so, but the way I felt something had to be going on. My mother immediately scheduled me for an appointment with my gynecologist. The following week I had the appointment and was informed I was officially pregnant. It's one thing to find out you're pregnant, but to have had my mother there was truly a horse of another color. I began to ask the doctor, "How could I be pregnant when I'm taking the pill?" The doctor stated, "Have you been sick?" I said, "Yes, I had a sinus infection and have been taking antibiotics." The doctor stated, "Then there is your reason. Since you were sick the antibiotics killed the potency of the birth control." All I could do was sit there because I already knew it was going to be a long ride home. I also knew once my father found out the horse would change colors again.

My mother said absolutely nothing, so I didn't know what to think. All I wanted to do was smoke some more and have a drink. I knew that wasn't the best option, but that was the only thing going through my mind at the time. The only other thing playing in my head was this same doctor told me I would never be able to have any children after the first pregnancy. When we made it to the house my mother was still not speaking to me and she called my father. My mother told my father, "You need to get home quick because we need to talk; it's about Denise." By the time my father made it home my mother was still not speaking to me. My mother asked me to go to my room while she talked to my father. I got up and went into my room and called

Ted to tell him I was pregnant. Ted was excited, and I was at a loss for words trying to figure out what was going on around me.

I was called back into the room and we all sat at the dining room table. My father stated, "You do know what this means right?" I replied "No, not really." My father stated, in his authoritative voice, "You are going to get married and that is the end of the discussion. Also call this Ted and tell him to come over here today so he knows what is going to take place." I was overwhelmed so I figured he would be too. I immediately called Ted and told him to get over to the house, so my parents could talk to him.

Ted made it to the house and the atmosphere was as cold as ice. It almost felt as if we were in the arctic because the tension and the stares were piercing. Ted spoke to both my parents and not a word was uttered by them. After about ten minutes, my father, in his authoritative voice again, stated, "Y'all are gonna get married and it will happen before Denise starts to show. There is no say in the matter and we will determine when the date will be." Both Ted and I looked at each other and said, "Okay".

Now I will give a little history; I've only known Ted for a period of three months, I found out I was pregnant in January, got married in March and had a baby in September; all in 1994. If it seems intense for you, just imagine living the scenario out. Honestly, I didn't kick my habit right away because I was only twenty and really didn't have a clue what was going on around me. I know smoking was not the best choice especially now I was pregnant, but I just needed to get away. The countdown began for something I wasn't ready for; a new life with a man I barely liked and being a mother all at the same time. I convinced myself I could eventually love Ted and hoped it would be worth my time.

6

FROM THE FRYING PAN TO THE FIRE

I was preparing myself for another roller coaster ride. Ted and I were told we were going to get married in March of 1994. Still trying to wrap my mind around all of this, I was then asked by my mother if I would consider having an abortion. This question was asked at least three other times and each time I told my mother I was not going to do it. I stated, "If God allowed this to happen then it was for a reason." At this point in my life, God was the farthest thing from my mind. If you would have asked me to spell God I wouldn't know how to do it. From that moment on I prepared myself to be a wife to a man I didn't even know.

It was now time for the wedding which was held in the backyard of my parents' house. Everyone was in attendance and it was a day I wish I could forget. It did feel good though to have everyone with their eyes on me and wishing me well. For once I could truly say life was taking a turn that might turn out to be something good for me. I would no longer be under my parents' roof, and having my own house might be a new start to making a change in the right direction. After all, I had such a terrible past; this could be the start of a new beginning. Or would it be? Only time would tell what life had in store for me as a wife and soon-to-be mother.

The day was over, and it was time for the new journey to begin. It was a shotgun wedding, so we didn't have a honeymoon, but instead we went to a hotel to spend the night and consummate the marriage. The night didn't go as planned because Ted was totally wasted, and nothing happened that night. I knew from that moment on I was forced into the biggest mistake of my life. I knew I didn't want to be married to him and I'm sure Ted felt the same. I was lying next to him snoring and I was trying to envision what married life would be like hoping it would be like the movies or even like the fairy tales I read as a child. Only time could tell what my disappointments would turn out to be and not knowing only made things worse.

After the first month of being married I received a true dose of medicine I couldn't bear to swallow. I had completely stopped all my bad habits because I knew it wasn't about me anymore but about the child I was carrying. I had noticed again why I disliked Ted in the first place and it showed daily and started to make me sick to my stomach. Ted had a ritual that he would follow to a tee and he made sure I followed it as well. Ted would keep a pint of Crown Royal in the freezer and a black canister of marijuana on the counter. I made the dreaded mistake one day and moved the canister and that was the start of the verbal abuse. Ted stated," If you ever touch my shit again it's going to be your ass." I made it my business to never move the canister to ensure he would never do anything to me. The entire pregnancy I wasn't sure what to think or feel since I didn't know if he was serious or not.

The apartment we stayed in was next door to a Latino family in Metairie. Metairie is a city which is the largest community in Jefferson Parish which is outside of New Orleans. Metairie is a part of a census-designated place (CDP) and is well populated and is unincorporated. Ted was already living there so it made sense for us to stay there. The lady next door was so wonderful, and we called her "Mama". Mama made sure to look in on me when Ted wasn't home. Ted was gone a lot and I had to find things to do to keep me busy since I wasn't working. Often, I was bored and remembered one night I watched OJ Simpson on the run for possibly killing his wife and for hours I was in front of the television alone. Ted worked at a restaurant after being fired from the shoe store for stealing merchandise. He was the only one working and after a while we could no longer afford the rent, so we talked about moving closer to my parents. Once the move took place, I wasn't prepared for what was coming next.

We moved to my parents' house, but only for a week since our new apartment wasn't ready, and I was getting close to my due date. The apartment was only ten minutes away and was close enough if I would go into labor. Ted changed jobs again and started working for a famous fast food restaurant and the pay was better. Ted started being a good husband and there weren't any complaints, but of course I spoke too prematurely.

September was here, and I was preparing for my son to be born. I got adjusted to being a wife and now to be a mother. My son decided to make a grand entrance weighing ten pounds and eight ounces. I never imagined from that moment on I would experience such a love and realized I had been looking in all the wrong places until then. Ted really stepped up to the plate and everything went smoothly for several months. I thought I finally had the opportunity to be happy even after all the hell I had been through. TJ made everything seem perfect even though there wasn't such a thing as perfect or at least not to my knowledge. I was happy for once in my life and I didn't want it to end and I didn't want to wake up either.

That all changed rather quickly and I was like a deer in the headlights.

We were settled in the apartment and Ted was still working at the fast food restaurant and things started to look up. Our relationship was going through some minor changes and now we were married for little over a year. I was home taking care of TJ and Ted was off work, but received a call to come in. Ted needed to take care of a matter since he was the store manager and left the apartment around 4:00pm. He told me he wouldn't be gone long so I didn't think anything of it. After several hours of not hearing from Ted I began calling and paging him to see what was going on. I had become frustrated by now and it was after midnight. I started to get scared and thought something might have happened to Ted. I was considering calling the police, but I knew several hours had to go by before something could be done. I was frantic thinking my son wouldn't have his father and only being married for over a year, I had made up my mind I was going to be a single parent.

It was 2 a.m. and I was completely frantic. I heard loud music, so I looked out the window and it was Ted pulling up in front of the apartment building. I became furious trying to figure out what lie he would come up with since he didn't answer all the pages and calls from me. Ted finally came into the apartment, but he never came into the bedroom. I heard the front door open, he had come up the steps and never turned the light on. The only light I saw had come from the refrigerator. I was so mad I got up not knowing my life would change forever. I walked to the front room and found Ted having sex with the cashier from the store he managed. When the girl looked up and saw me she took Ted's car keys and left. Ted was so drunk I started to fight him and before I knew it I pushed him down the steps. The apartment was on the second floor and the stairs were on the inside which led to the entrance. While he was down there, I grabbed TJ and left the apartment. I finally made it to my parents' house and told my mother what happened between Ted and the cashier. After I cried my eyes out, I was told by my mother, "You need to go back because men need to get certain things out of their system and that child needs his daddy." So, I listened to my mother and went back home. When I got home Ted asked, "What happened and where is my car?" Once I had calmed down I told Ted all that happened. My marriage was never the same and what made things worse, I stayed.

7

WAKING UP FROM THE NIGHTMARE

For months, I felt trapped and had to watch what I did when dealing with Ted. I started praying my situation would get better, but instead it only got worse. As the weeks went on, Ted's behavior only spiraled out of control and his actions allowed his words to have no weight. After the incident with the girl from the restaurant, Ted felt he could do whatever he wanted, and my life was now in his hands. For months, I had to do what he wanted and what I wanted didn't matter since I was his wife.

We eventually moved out of the apartment to a duplex which was a few blocks from the apartment complex. I thought with the move maybe I would have a chance to start over and maybe, Ted would see what he was doing and change his ways. When we moved to the duplex, I was the only one working, but Ted was resourceful and landed back on his feet. Ted started working at a car dealership, only after befriending two of the men on the street who also worked at the dealership. I was happy I didn't have to work as much as I did, but as always, I was wrong. I keep hoping I might get the start "over" I was looking for but that was one "hope" that would never come true.

Things went well for a while and we even got along, which was surprising to me. For once things were going in the right direction and I was going to enjoy it for as long as it lasted. We started attending a local church and after a few months we both were baptized. I thought things would be great after we were baptized. Ted was acting like he had sense, but there was another twist to the equation. My mother was quite angry I left Catholicism since I grew up Catholic. Again, who would have thought after twenty-three years of being Catholic I would make such a bold move? I didn't see the problem; my mother grew up Baptist and she remained Baptist until she married my father.

My parents were married in the 1970s and once married my mother converted over to Catholicism. So why was it such a problem; the world may never know? God will give some thorns and it's still here poking me in my side to this very day.

I was back in college full time and I worked two jobs. Ted was only concerned about looking good on the showroom floor, so my paychecks covered the bills. Ted only got paid once a month, and his only concern was to make sure his suit game was on point. I mean, he had to look good on the sales floor. I didn't mind because he was leaving me alone and I had some peace or at least I thought. Ted's new behavior lasted only for a brief time when old habits returned.

Ted was selling cars, so he figured he would try to keep up with the Jones'. He had become good friends with Adam who was one of the men on the block. Adam had been working at the dealership for a while, so he would lease his cars. Adam leased a new Maxima and Ted decided to do the same. Ted couldn't afford the lease, so he got a used Maxima instead. I made it home from work with TJ and I thought Ted had someone at the house, but it turned out to be him and he didn't tell me anything. Ted was excited and told me I couldn't drive it since the car was his, even though Adam had a new model Maxima, but Ted didn't care. All he wanted to do was to keep up with his new group of friends. Adam was a bad influence and Ted wanted to do everything Adam did, and it was causing friction between us. Ted would be out all night and didn't care how I felt about it. Adam was single, and Ted didn't want to be married in the first place. Adam's lifestyle appealed to Ted, and it showed in his demeanor. For months, Ted would come home late and didn't include TJ or me in his daily plans. I felt as if I was in this by myself. Everything had become overwhelming and I was starting to think that I was the problem. I spent a lot of time by myself, so I had a lot of time to process what had been taking place around me. I realized I wanted my son, but did I really need all the drama that came along with it. I started suffering from depression and I spent most of my time in bed. I tried to pull myself out of it, but being around Ted only made things worse and to add insult to injury, he treated me like I was a child.

As I shared earlier, I was working two jobs and it was time for me to prepare for graduation. I was trying my best to stay focused, but it didn't work out as I hoped it would. I was working at a group home allowing me to channel my negative energy and not think about what I was experiencing at home. TJ was young, and he didn't realize what was going on around him. I was glad because I couldn't explain even if I wanted to. I wished I could wake up from this nightmare, but it only intensified as the months and years went on. This roller coaster ride was both interesting and heart-wrenching and I didn't have the words to describe these unwanted feelings.

While working at the group home I tried my best to spend as much time there as possible, so I wouldn't have to go home. I had a deal worked out with the babysitter allowing TJ to spend the majority of his time at her house. Between the babysitter and my parents, TJ would be taken care of with no problems. I tried my best to protect TJ from his father's actions and since I was the only one being a parent I had to do the best I knew how. Vehemently my actions allowed Ted to be who he was and there wasn't a way to change him so there was nothing I could do.

I found myself always sleeping but I was available to make sure TJ was taken care of especially when Ted wasn't around. It got to the point I would rely on the team at the group home to help me work through my feelings since I couldn't rely on anyone else. I was tired, but I knew I couldn't give up and TJ was depending on me to be there for him. I was just going through the motions and felt I was living a mundane life with nowhere to go or even a way out. I started to question why I was going through all of this and I didn't have the answers to the questions I was asking. I started falling deeper and deeper into depression but continued to pull myself up when I went to work. Ironically, working gave me a sense of belonging. I was told by Ted on several occasions he would rather be in the streets than home with me so working seemed like a better alternative. If I could just live at work then the world would be a better place, but reality would set in and I had to go home.

Ted started his controlling ways again which caused me to shut down. I was studying for school and had to get permission to leave the house often. I needed to pick up some books from a classmate and he had to make sure the person was female before letting me out of the house. After he talked to my classmate, I was able to leave. Ted told me after I got the books to pick up a beer from the store for him. I made it back home but forgot to get the beer. Ted took a hot pot off the stove and threw it at me. Ted said, "You are so stupid, and I don't understand why you're even in school when you couldn't follow simple directions." The pot hit the wall and he pushed me down telling me I needed to clean up the mess. Ted was cooking mustard greens and it was all over the carpet. I had to find something else to fix for dinner but was scared to even ask, at this point. Ted made it seem like it was all my fault because he didn't get his beer. I finally figured out something to eat for dinner, but he refused to let me eat since he was angry. I was okay with it and I went to bed early after losing my appetite.

My life felt like an endless nightmare I couldn't wake up from. For months, I did what I could for me and TJ by avoiding Ted as much as possible. Every morning I would get up making sure TJ was ready for the babysitter and I went to work. I'd been working at the group home for a while and I moved up to supervisor. It happened by default since everyone else continued to quit. Graduation was getting close and I couldn't afford to look for another job. I was the morning supervisor and it worked out fine, so I could focus on graduating. As long as I worked I didn't have to think about anything and sleeping was the only way to avoid talking to Ted, especially if he thought I was asleep.

Graduation was getting closer and being the morning supervisor made me feel like I had accomplished something. Everyone listened to me and I didn't realize something that simple made a difference. Remember, I wasn't getting attention at home, so it felt good for a change. The team members continued to quit, and I was now responsible for bringing in new staff members. I interviewed so many people, but I never knew I would run into someone who would change my life drastically. This person made going to work worth my time and his being around made things better. Chase was hired to work at the group home and I was extremely happy. Over time, our work relationship turned into more than I expected. To ensure my time with Chase was well spent, I made sure Chase worked the morning shift with me.

8

FALLING IN LOVE FOR THE FIRST TIME

Working with Chase was a new experience for me since I never knew what love truly was, and the way he made me feel good. My relationship with Ted only got worse and being at work helped me deal with the pain. Being around Chase allowed me to be myself and he understood exactly who I was. Several months had passed and this was when I learned that Chase meant more to me than I ever could imagine. I received a call that gave me mixed feelings and Chase was there to help me through the incident. He proved through his actions he was the type of man I needed to be around.

I received a call that Ted was in jail and there was nothing I could do about it. We didn't have any money saved up, so I had to call his relatives and friends to see if they could help get him out of jail. Part of me was excited he was in jail, but the other part knew I had to do something. In the process, I called Chase and he talked me through what I needed to do to get Ted out of jail. I was intrigued because for one he knew my situation, and two, he helped me with my problem. This spoke volumes and impressed me at the same time.

I made sure Ted would get out of jail the next day, so I called Chase back and we talked until the morning. I was confused because he knew I was married, but he empathized with my situation. That night I explained to Chase all I had been through and he still wanted to be there for me and this continued to impress me even more. I couldn't believe how amazing he was, especially when I was dealing with my situation of being in a terrible marriage.

When I made it to work the next day Chase was extremely supportive, and it put a smile on my face. Things started to get more interesting between the two of us and everyone started to notice. We were spending more time together and I started to enjoy it to the point that Ted started to notice how happy I was. Being with Chase made me feel good and it was different from the way I was treated by Ted. At this point in my life I realized that I was with someone who wanted to see me happy and I got joy out of more than just being a mother.

It was time for graduation and I couldn't be happier. This was a long time coming and I knew after graduation there would be more out there for me and my life could go in another direction. The day of graduation I was informed by Ted he didn't want me to go back to school because he didn't need to be with someone smarter than him. As we were on our way to the graduation, his statement bothered me and made me want to go even more. Remember, everything my parents told me not to do, I did it to piss them off, so I decided to do the same with him. Going back to school would be a way to piss Ted off and after graduation it was on my agenda. Who knows, he might even consider leaving me and I would be fine with it if he did and then I could be with Chase for sure.

Things continued to get worse with my relationship with Ted, and being with Chase was the only solace I had. When I wasn't with Chase I put all my energy and time into my son. I would find ways to spend time with Chase. I knew I was caught up though when I found myself driving to a part of town

I wasn't familiar with. New Orleans was uniquely divided between two sides of the Mississippi River and going across the western side of the river was a whole new world for me. I took a chance and agreed to see Chase across the river, so I had to come up with something to tell Ted. I told Ted I needed to go to the store and would be back in a few hours. Ted then questioned, "Why are you going to be gone so long and you need to be back because I'm not watching TJ all night." I told him I wouldn't be, but in my mind, I didn't know how long it would take. Once I made it across the river I didn't have a clue where I was going, but I knew Chase wouldn't send me somewhere to hurt me.

I called Chase to let him know I made it to the spot he told me to meet him and in less than five minutes he was there. More and more I knew I had found someone who truly wanted to be with me and I needed to find a way to get out of this terrible situation I was in. I told

Chase about what Ted said and he said, "I'll make sure that you will be back in time, so nothing will happen to you or TJ." I was in awe because for once I had someone willing to make sure I was safe. This was the true meaning of action versus just saying words. I never knew what love meant, but Chase was trying to introduce it to me. I only spent about an hour with him, but it was the best hour of my life. Chase made sure I had an amazing time and I didn't want it to end. He assured me we would spend more time with each other and he understood my situation. Chase tried not to make me feel worse than what I was experiencing in my relationship with Ted.

I made it back home and Ted asked, "Why are you smiling?" before he left out of the door for the evening. This was normal for him since he would spend all his time away from the house anyway. Ted would say all the time, "I'm going out to see what I'm missing so I could come home to you." I didn't care since Chase had me smiling on the inside and I felt as if life really mattered for once. Don't get me wrong, I love my son, but it felt good to have someone show me some love for once. After Ted left the house, I stayed on the phone with Chase until it was time to go to work. The morning had come, and I had enough energy to get TJ ready for the babysitter and me for work. I didn't feel tired, but had a new-found energy after being depressed for so long. In my mind, I had another opportunity to get it right, but there was one problem, I was still married.

Ted continued to go out more and more leaving me home with TJ. I didn't care because I had someone who wanted to be with me and I wasn't lonely. I was married for two years and this prison sentence just seemed to spiral out of control with no end. Chase made my nights bearable and after a while I stopped even thinking about the foolishness Ted was doing. All I knew was I was happy, and I didn't care what Ted was doing as long as it didn't interfere with my happiness.

There were many lonely nights and I found ways to see Chase without it stopping me from being a mother. I always made sure TJ was cared for but spending time with Chase made me feel like sunshine and that carried over to TJ. My mind was put to ease knowing TJ wasn't old enough to know what was going on yet or to understand the abuse I experienced at the hand of his father. I didn't understand why I was going through this, but it must have been for a reason, because if it was up to me I would have never experienced this journey in my life.

Things started looking up for me and I learned how to tune out the negativity that took place at home. I even set it up, so that we would only be around each other for short periods of time so I would have peace. This went on for months and it was as if he was good with it too. My life didn't feel so mundane anymore, and I was able to tolerate my present situation with Chase being in the picture. Ted didn't care about me and the feeling was mutual. With him not coming home most nights, I was able to come up with ways to spend more time with Chase. The best thing was we worked together, making it a plus in my book. I could say I did experience love, but it would be put to the test with one simple move. This next move proved the reason I knew I had to make a change in my life.

I had gotten used to being at home and there were times when I wished he'd never come home again, but it never happened. Ted went out as usual and the next morning changed my life forever. This would have never been the journey for my life, but it was part of a bigger picture that both included and excluded at the same time. It may sound funny, but you will understand why it was said soon.

9

ANSWERING THE CALL

Ted had been out all night with his brother and they had come in around 6:00 am in the morning. I was dressed and had made sure TJ was dressed too. The house we lived in had stairs underneath the carport which led into the apartment. These steps were different because it had carpet and metal stripping on each one. I opened the door that morning to confront him about coming home late and he pushed past me. As he went into the house with his brother right behind him, I stayed outside on the steps. When I called his name, Ted turned around and pushed me down the steps. I slid down the steps with the front side of my body hitting each step. The socks I had on made the fall more dangerous, and I had bruises from head to toe. Ted's brother, Tyrone, had come out to check on me, but I couldn't move. I wished, at that point, that I was dead.

Tyrone asked, "Do you need me to call the police?" Ted told Tyrone to come in the house and to leave me out there. Tyrone went back into the house, but he then came back later to ask if he could help me up and asked again if he needed to call for an ambulance. I told him to just leave me alone and that I would get up on my own. I also told Tyrone, "You don't care so why act like you do? Go and play with your brother." I lost all signs of hope and knew God needed to take my life because if this was what I had to deal with, it wasn't worth it.

After laying on the steps for a while I guessed I had become delusional from all the pain. I remember crying out to God and telling Him, "Just take my life", since I didn't want to live any more. As sure as you are reading this now, I could hear God say to me then, "No my child, I have too much for you to do." Well like any unpleasant situation we find ourselves in, I told God, "If You will get me out of this situation I will do whatever You need me to do."

Trust me, He held me to it. When I was finally able to get up I knocked on the door and Tyrone let me back in the house. I asked Tyrone, "Where is your brother?" and he stated, "He's sleeping, and I'm sorry that my brother didn't do anything to help you". I informed Tyrone, "All that doesn't matter, and I need to get TJ to the babysitter and I need to get to work." Tyrone said, "You crazy." I told him, "I don't care, and me staying here is only going to make things worse, so I need to leave for work."

After the incident, I called my mother and she said, "You can't come over because if your father sees you he will go to jail, so do the best you can to resolve the issue." From that moment on, I knew my mother and I would never be on the same page and she showed me where I stood with her. I hung up the phone, dropped TJ off at the babysitter and I made it to the group home. My concern was to figure out what I was going to tell Chase about what happened.

When I got to work, I explained why I was late to the other Supervisor. I told him I was having car trouble and I had to wait for someone to help me change the tire. The other Supervisor, Alvin, knew something was wrong, and he was giving me the opportunity to explain. Alvin informed, "Chase called in sick and when you didn't come in right away I thought that something was wrong." I told Alvin, "I'm good and I just had a flat tire. I promise there's nothing wrong." I didn't care that I was being questioned by Alvin, and I was at ease knowing Chase wasn't coming to work. I could always handle Alvin, but Chase knew my situation and he would have done something to Ted which would be far worse.

It was getting close to the end of the shift and Alvin called me into the office to talk. Once in the office, Alvin questioned me again about what happened that morning. He said, "I do recognize the warning signs of being abused. Do you need to go to the emergency room?" I told Alvin, "I'll be fine and all I need is some time to heal." Alvin then said, "You know if

Chase would have come to work he would have definitely done something to remedy the matter." I was glad Chase didn't come in and hopefully I would feel better before the day was over. I told Alvin, "Please don't call the police. I will be fine; I promise." Alvin said, "You better do something with your face since it's changing colors-this is why I called you in the office." I looked in the mirror and my chin was turning purple so I definitely had to think of something quick, so that I wouldn't draw attention to myself.

After getting TJ from the babysitter, I drove around hoping that when I got home Ted wouldn't be there. Once I made it to the house I called Tyrone to see where his brother was, and he told me he was with him, so the situation wouldn't get worse. I informed him that I was fine and to make sure he didn't come back until I was able to get myself back on track.

Remember my face was bruised and being light-skinned didn't help any. I left the house with TJ to get some makeup to cover the bruises, but I knew it wouldn't last long since this wasn't something I normally did. I was still trying to wrap my mind around why this was happening to me. I tried to sleep after I got TJ in bed, knowing Ted wasn't coming home. Maybe some rest would do me good and when I woke up it could have all been a bad dream. Plus, in the morning I would need to explain to Chase what happened, and I needed a very good story to tell.

The next morning, I started my day as usual, but instead I had to put on makeup. I got to work thinking it was going to be a normal day, but it didn't turn out to be the case. Chase said, "Can you please come into the conference room?" I already knew why he was calling me in there and it was because of Alvin. Chase mentioned, "I was told about what happened yesterday. Why didn't you call me?!" Again, this man had shown me something I had never experienced before, and it felt good. I never realized I started the process of answering God's call and it only took for me to go down a flight of steps to realize it.

This was only the beginning and there was more to come as I walked into this calling on my life. Chase was a vital part and I don't think he knew it either, but he was the important piece for me to take the initial step. I didn't have a relationship with Christ and what I was doing as a married woman was definitely not what a called person was supposed to do. If you think about it, all of this started with me dealing with a married man in the first place. Remember, God takes the broken to help other broken people to heal. I guess I was the best at what I did and did qualify to help others in the same position. God doesn't need us for anything, but He does see the best in us during our sin. Again, going down a flight of steps didn't make me come towards God, it only made me run further away and I ran until I couldn't run anymore.

10

TRASH DAY

ell I hope you're enjoying the ride so far, because there's still more to come. Just like a cat, I would always land back on my feet. Things calmed down between me and Ted as we prepared for another move. In a brief period of time we moved out of Orleans parish and to Jefferson parish. I almost felt like a fugitive on the run and yes, I kept on running. Louisiana always did things a little differently. We are known for having parishes instead of counties.

Initially, Louisiana was under the rule of both France and Spain and the boundaries coincided with church parishes. Over time, Louisiana never deviated from using the original term. Now back to the apartment, I'm not sure how Ted found it, but as always, I was looking for a clean slate. I liked the new apartment in Metairie and it was extremely huge for a two-bedroom. (It's pronounced MET-a-ree, for those wondering.)

TJ was around the age of four when I applied for graduate school as I had promised. Ted and I both started working a new job together by this time. Yes, I said it, together. We worked at a popular home security company and it was kind of strange working together again. Ted was a salesman and I was the manager of telemarketing, working in the evenings. Things went south for him at the dealership and I had left the library and the group home. With all that took place, it was as if I was running trying to find innovative ways to reinvent myself for some sanity. Here was where I met one of my best friends, and to this day she's still hanging in there. Ironically enough, Shawny and I went to college together, but made the connection later at work. Shawny and I would talk all the time, and she made it clear she didn't like Ted. I ignored her because I knew I couldn't get out of that hole even if I tried.

A few months had passed and I was starting to enjoy being at the job. Since Ted worked at night I was able to have some peace. It was sweet, and my mother was watching TJ, so I didn't have any concerns. I was the only African-American female manager and things started to get interesting at work. The roller coaster ride continued and quite frankly, I was getting tired of it. I couldn't talk to Ted about the situation, but Shawny did her best to tell me how to handle the matter appropriately.

Stanley was my immediate supervisor, and Jonah was the regional manager. There were two locations in the state, and my position was a move in the right direction, or at least I thought it was. I had to report directly to Stanley, but this particular day Jonah called me into his office. Jonah informed me, "You will be working closely with me and it will be many late nights with the door closed and no one needs to know about this." Now remember I told you when I was younger it was told to me that this only happened to pretty girls. I just looked at Jonah and said, "Okay". I knew in my mind this wasn't going to start again and especially not with a white man.

I started doing all I could to avoid Jonah and did my best to avoid telling Ted. It wasn't like he was going to do anything anyway, but I didn't want the hassle at home now that things were going well for a change. When I would run across Jonah I would make sure there were a lot of people around, so he wouldn't confront me. This lasted for two weeks and the unexpected happened. It was never a dull moment with me and this was when I felt like the trash that sat by the door ready to be put out.

I would always bring TJ to the babysitter in the morning and then I would go to work. This particular morning was different. To my surprise, I was told by the receptionist that Stanley needed to see me immediately. I went into his office and Stanley said demandingly, "I had some leads on my desk and I was told that you moved them. If I don't have them in the next thirty minutes you will be fired. Do you understand me?" I panicked because I didn't have a clue of what Stanley was talking about. I scampered trying to find the lead I was told I took. I started to believe I may have taken them and forgotten where they were. It didn't help that I lost ten minutes trying to think where they could be.

In the middle of the confusion, one of the sales representatives, Louis, pulled me on the side and asked, "Were these the leads Stanley was talking about?" I told Louis, "I'm not sure", since I had never seen them before. Louis proceeded to say, "I was told by Jonah to get them off Stanley's desk and that's what I did, and I will bring them back to Stanley and let him know what happened." I told Louis, "Thank you" and sat down to gather my thoughts.

I felt like I needed to be back in the tub of Palmolive and I was starting to feel like the trash sitting in the sun for a while.

After Louis left Stanley's office I was called back in. The words which were said left a scar that hasn't healed to this day. Stanley said, "Let's just dust this under the rug and never talk about it again and you could just go back to work and I'm here if you need me." I was dumb-founded because I was told in a matter of thirty minutes I would be unemployed and now it was "Have a wonderful day!" Did I miss the memo? I couldn't say anything because I didn't have a clue what had just happened.

I was now called into Jonah's office and I was terrified by what was about to take place.

Jonah said, "I told you I was in control, and since you wanted to avoid me I had to show you I'm the boss. If you don't do what I say it will only get worse for you." I was really scared because I didn't know what to do. I called Shawny on the phone to find out when she was coming into the office, and waited until she got there to talk. It appeared to be the longest day of my life and it was only 11:00 am and I had to be there until 9:00 pm.

I was visibly shaken up and the receptionist asked me to come to her office. Ms. Alice was an amazing woman and she felt like a mother figure to me. Ms. Alice asked me to explain and I did. After I told, Ms. Alice said, "This isn't the first time this has happened, and it probably won't be the last with Jonah." Ms. Alice shared, "Jonah got the position only because of family and he thinks he can deal with people anyway he wants to." Ms. Alice stated," Baby we gon' pray about it and God will work it out." I just looked at Ms. Alice and then put my head back down. What was going through my mind was why God kept letting all these things happen to me, and was I such a bad person for it to happen to?

When Shawny made it to work I was still with Ms. Alice. Ms. Alice shared with Shawny what took place and Shawny said, "It's funny that this situation has come up again." Shawny stated, "I heard that Jonah had done the same thing to a blonde in Baton Rouge and she recorded everything, and she called Jonah out on it." I told Shawny that it didn't matter, and since I was the only black person they wouldn't take me seriously, so I should just quit. I set out to do it, and I found a job working at a popular bank in New Orleans. Since I was treated like trash I took it upon myself to take "me" out of the equation. I only stayed at the job another month, and then moved on to the banking job.

When leaving the job at the alarm company, I told Ted I needed to do something different and it would allow me to be home for TJ. Ted was fine initially with the decision, knowing he spent minimal time with TJ anyway. Ted had thought I was up to something and started to have me followed. I was still seeing Chase and being followed only made things crazy for us both. I had an idea I was being followed, but I pushed it to the back of my mind as much as possible. Who would ever admit their life was a plethora of movies all tied into one. I never did, but it was an ongoing story line I wished I was getting paid for.

I enjoyed working at the bank. I worked in customer service and it was a consistent break from being around Ted. The job only required me to work Monday through Friday, which allowed me to clear my head and spend more time with TJ. TJ was turning four and watching him grow was my heart's desire. I had been working at the bank for about six months now and working there gave me a sense of belonging. Things had been going well at home, but only for a little while. Months had passed then Ted went back to his old ways. The honeymoon experience was nothing new to me. I may not have taken a honeymoon initially, but I'd experienced the "Honeymoon" phase far too often. In the social work realm, the "Honeymoon" phase usually would last from a period of six months to a year. This was the normal roller coaster ride between the two of us. The "Honeymoon" phase is when things would get really bad and the abuser would state they didn't mean to do it and they were sorry for what they did, and it would never happen again. This had become the norm and I would know when it was about to start, knowing Ted's predictable behaviors. Things shifted again, and Ted always kept me on my toes.

As I was preparing for work one morning Ted told me he would bring me to work and drop TJ off at the babysitter. I didn't have a problem with it as it gave me a break from paying to park. My day went well, but there was a slight change when I got off. Ted had picked me up in a different car, so I questioned, "What happened?" Ted informed me, "I got rid of your car and I got you a new Maxima." I was trying to figure out why we needed another car, but I never had a say with anything, so the new car was now incorporated into my life. For several weeks Ted would drop me off at work and bring TJ to the babysitter. I was confused as to why he was doing this. I mean, I knew how to drive, and I was fine with bringing TJ to the babysitter. So why did Ted suddenly need to chauffeur me around? Little did I know, there was another shift about to occur in my life. It was the weekend and Ted did his best to start another fight and the "Honeymoon" phase started all over again. I didn't do something he wanted, and he locked me out of the apartment. I was left outside without a phone or any shoes, so I just sat on the step for hours. A neighbor passing by asked, "Are you okay?". I said yes, that I was just sitting to clear my head and I needed a little break, but couldn't go far because of my son. I couldn't tell the neighbor I was locked out. Ted eventually let me back in and I was convinced he was truly crazy.I felt like trash again, and I had nowhere to go. Sitting outside had me thinking I was waiting for the garbage man to come to pick me up on the normal scheduled days.

It was Monday again, and I would be dropped off for work with no means of fending for myself. I was only given enough money to eat and I was told I better not tell anyone what was going on with me. My mind started to cave in, and thinking of my son was my way of keeping my sanity. I wasn't sure what was going on with Ted, but he had reverted to treating me like a child. I was alienated from everyone around me. I was still seeing Chase, but I had to be strategic when dealing with him.

Ted's aggression had escalated to the point that he was calling the job daily and questioning who was coming to see me at work. My supervisor, Floyd, called me into his office and asked, "What is going on with you? I'm concerned about you." I told Floyd, "My husband is having a bad day", and

I apologized for him calling so much. I finally went back to my cubicle because I didn't know what to expect next.

Ted continued to work, but I couldn't understand what was going on with him, and frankly I didn't care. I just wanted him to leave me alone while I was at work. The abuse escalated, but it was more emotional and verbal than anything else. I told Ted, "I would rather you hit me because the bruises would go away, but the things you say are what sticks around forever." I was trying to understand what I did wrong in my life to deserve all this drama. It was a constant roller coaster ride and I was only concerned about TJ. If something happened to me, who would take care of TJ and give him what's best? This was a constant thought as I lived in a situation not fit for an animal.

The madness went on for several weeks and each day Ted would drop me off at work without keys or a phone, and with just enough money for lunch. I would look forward to work, but didn't do a decent job once I was there. I worked in customer service and I followed the same routine daily. Once I clocked in, I would log in to have the calls routed to my desk. When the call reached my que, I would watch it drop and then I would put the customer back on hold again. I had become a pro at it and did this for weeks until Floyd called me back into his office. Floyd stated, "Denise what is going on? I see that you haven't answered a call in about two weeks and this is grounds for you to be terminated." I got nervous and shared with Floyd what was going on with me and how Ted was treating me. Floyd replied, "I will see what I can do so you won't lose your job." I was grateful because I didn't need more drama to deal with.

Over the months I had befriended two women at the job. I would speak to everyone, but these two made the day go by faster. They helped me not to think about all the negativity I was dealing with. Their names were Cyan and Amanda. I would have lunch with them and eventually share what was going on at home. I felt guilty about telling people what I was going through, but it also felt good to get it off my chest. It was as if talking about it made it seem like it was happening to someone else and not me. It felt good not feeling like trash or needing to soak in Palmolive for a change. And the best part, I wasn't being judged for my actions.

The next few months had become routine, but I was able to talk about how I felt, and I started to feel good. I was still being dropped off as well as being picked up, but I was feeling better about what was going on around me. Ted shared, "I need to know where you are at all times, so I don't have to worry about what you're doing without knowing first." I was trapped, and I couldn't make any moves without getting permission first. I couldn't believe my life had gotten down to this and there was absolutely nothing I could do about it.

I was given permission to go to the store and when I returned Ted was at the apartment with three females. I walked back outside to make sure I was at the right place. Tyrone said, "Hey sis-in-law. These are some of my friends and we were about to go hang out". Ted just looked at me and never said a word. Tyrone stated, "We are going to get Daniel now that he's out of jail." Daniel was a twin and was in jail for drug possession. Tyrone asked, "Sis, can you move the car? Thanks." As I was getting into the car Ted mumbled, "Don't wait up since I don't know when I will be home." I was cool with it and hoped he would never come home as always. Unfortunately, he did come back home, and the nightmare just continued.

Several months passed and I was faced with yet another situation I wasn't prepared for. Daniel, the youngest brother, had been released from jail and I had no clue of who he was. I never knew what was going on in Ted's family, but it was a huge pill to swallow when I did find out. I was home alone with the television on and getting TJ ready for bed. I was listening to the news and heard a black male was on the run for killing his wife. I jokingly made a comment, "It sounds like some dumb shit that Ted would do" and I put TJ to bed during the commercials. Once the news had come back on I started screaming when I saw Daniel's face on the screen. TJ came running in the room and when he saw me crying he began to cry too. In a panic, I called Ted to tell him what was going on. Ted stated, "You better let him in and if you don't then you will have hell to pay." I was now scared because Daniel was on the run and could show up at any time. I immediately checked all the doors and locked me and TJ in the bedroom because I didn't know what to do if Daniel showed up.

It was after midnight and I didn't hear anything, so I figured we would be alright. I got up and put TJ back in his bed, but I double checked the doors first. More time had passed making it after 3:00 am. I stayed up praying nothing would happen to us. Around 4:30 am Ted finally made it home and he was in a horrible mood. I started thinking I needed to make a move soon because I didn't know what would happen next.

Ted was drunk, and his anger overtook him with rage. He forced me to have sex with him and when it was over he told me what had happened after our phone call. Ted mentioned Daniel contacted their other brother Damon on the phone and explained the entire situation of what happened between him and his wife. Damon then said that Daniel swore he wasn't going back to jail and shot himself in the head while they were on the phone. Ted then shared that Daniel had only been out of jail for a few weeks and decided to go on the Lakefront with his new wife. The Lakefront was a popular hangout spot in New Orleans and it tended to be heavily populated on the weekends. Daniel didn't recognize the man his wife hugged, which turned out to be her cousin, and got mad and shot her in the head later that night. After shooting her in the head he told everyone she left him, after he had rolled her body up in a carpet and threw her body in an abandoned area. Ted mentioned again how Daniel decided to commit suicide as well as how he blew his brains out. Ted said, "Me and Tyrone went to the site and identified the body and shit was hard to deal with." Ted said the most bizarre thing which stuck in my head. He said, "You do some dumb shit sometimes that would make me shoot you in the head too. You lucky I don't have a gun right now because you would be dead right now." If that wasn't the kicker, it caused me to think of my next move which was to leave him for good. I wasn't going to be considered trash anymore and I didn't need Ted to put me there permanently.

11

THE OTHER SIDE OF LONELY

I t was 1999 and the loneliest moment in my life, knowing my husband wanted to kill me if he had the chance. I continued to do my normal routine of working and caring for TJ, but the only difference now was thinking of a plan to get away from Ted. He would make it easy for me when he would go out of town to Las Vegas in October. I figured it would be the opportune time, and I had at least four months to get my plan together. I told Chase what I planned, and he informed me I should tell my parents, so the transition would be smoother. I knew I was tired and ready to leave Ted before he made the decision for me.

It was getting closer to October and Ted was leaving for Las Vegas the week of Halloween. I didn't celebrate the holiday, but I remembered it because it was my grandfather's birthday.

Also, on "All Souls Day", which is November 1st, my parents would go to the cemetery to put flowers on the graves for my grandparents. I told my parents about Ted's brother and my parents agreed I needed to leave him. I was angry initially because all the other times my mother didn't do anything, but it took for someone to get killed before she wanted to step in and help.

I didn't care anymore, and I started coming up with ways to leave. The plan was to act normal and when Ted left for Las Vegas I would move all my things out of the apartment. I spent a lot of time with Chase and we planned to start a life together. The thought made what I was going through easier to bear. I was extremely glad TJ was still too young, and being four was a way to protect him from all the hurt I experienced.

The entire week he was gone, I would ignore the calls which made him angry. One night he left several threatening messages on the voicemail and when I would go home, I noticed there were over twenty messages. I didn't think it could hold so many and it could have been more, but the tape ran out on the answering machine. I would only go home to check on the apartment then leave back out. I knew if I did check I would get angry and I enjoyed not seeing or dealing with him. This allowed me to embrace the peace I had, even if it was only for a few more days. Moving back to my parents would be a far better situation for me and TJ, but I knew I had to start somewhere.

I decided if I could get through the next few days I would get past the loneliness and have a chance to be happy. Chase and I talked about all the wonderful things we would do together, and I was looking forward to the day it would finally come. I figured I hadn't been happy all this time. Why not wait a few more months and possibly it could happen. It was my saving grace as I counted down to his return. Chase was always around and that made what I was going through easier to deal with.

It was finally time for Ted to come home. My parents and I picked him up from the airport.

My father figured we all would go together. We got to the apartment and TJ wouldn't get out. That was the plan, but it didn't turn out that way. Ted made it to the van and I pretended to be excited to see him. He talked the entire time about how much fun he had in Las Vegas and I was thinking about all the women he had been with. While talking, he even made a joke of wanting to go back and staying there. We made it to the apartment and Ted got out first. He told me to do the same and I didn't move. This time he yelled, "Get out of the van."

My father told Ted, "Son, she's not getting out of the van. Now go inside and let us go." Then we left him at the apartment.

Ted realized what was going on and he got in his car and started following us. He tried several times to run us off the road hoping to cause an accident. When we went to my parents' house, I tried to get some rest, but it never happened. It constantly stayed on my mind not knowing what Ted would do next. After all, he was a ticking time bomb waiting to go off. The entire time we were together I never had the opportunity to "learn" Ted, so his next move was never calculated. All I needed to do was make it to Monday then things would start looking up. My parents already had a lawyer in mind and the process to divorce Ted would begin.

I survived the weekend so that meant that the next stop was the lawyer's office. My father made it up in his mind that I was going to get divorced and he was going to pay for it. This was the best news ever since I didn't have any money. We made it to the lawyer's office and my father gave the tape of the voicemails to the lawyer. The lawyer was amazed by what he heard, and he stated, "I have had clients leave their husbands for less and you endured this daily." All I could do was say, "Yes." I felt like I was in a bubble under water because I couldn't hear anything that was said to me. I was focusing more on what to do next and not listening to how I should handle Ted in the next few months. The lawyer told my father what I needed to do until the divorce was finalized. It started to feel real that I was preparing to divorce Ted and I could have a clean slate on life.

There was never a time I wasn't on a roller coaster and it was going up to make the next drop. My grandfather was terminally ill, and the family had to prepare for his death. It was inevitable, but his passing still hurt a great deal. So much was going on at one time and it almost felt like I was being buried alive. Divorcing Ted and preparing for a funeral, what more could I handle?! Well the night before the funeral, Chase decided to take me out, so I could clear my head. In the car we decided to go back to his house to pick up something before heading to the movies. Unfortunately, things didn't go according to plan. We were joking around and got hit from behind. The impact of the hit was so strong that the car hit the guardrail. Chase checked to see if I was okay and then he approached the driver. The driver of the other vehicle must have been drunk or high because Chase couldn't make out anything the driver was saying. Chase told me to call 911 while he stopped the driver from leaving the scene. The police showed up to the scene and the officer stated, "The two of you are lucky that the car didn't go over the side of the bridge." Again, I questioned what was going on around me and why I was being punished. The funeral was the next morning and we decided not to say anything to my parents which would cause them to have a meltdown behind what happened. I made myself a promise not to say anything, ensuring it didn't take away from my grandfather passing. We promised to keep the accident between the two of us for as long as we could.

Several months went by and Ted refused to sign the divorce papers. He did it on purpose, but why, he didn't want me in the first place. The roller coaster circled several more times to the point I wanted to throw up from being so nauseous. It was as if I was pregnant again because it took nine months for the divorce to be final. When the papers were finally signed the occasion was joyful for another reason and not one of birth. The other side of loneliness took a turn in the right direction with the divorce being final the day before my birthday. It allowed me to have a clean slate when looking at the age of 27. I never imagined my birthday would be the second time around in the same life.

12

IN A GREAT SPACE

My relationship with Chase had grown stronger, or at least I thought. What I experienced next in my life posed a strain on the relationship as time progressed. Since I was a teenager, I would always suffer with my menstrual cycle and it had become the bane of my existence. In 1999, I was diagnosed with endometriosis. Endometriosis is a disorder where tissue grows outside of the uterus and it tends to be extremely painful. Ted would always tell me, "You're damaged goods and no man will ever want to be with you." After being diagnosed, I tried my best to deal with the pain and over time put a wedge between me and Chase. I did my best to keep the pain from him knowing I couldn't have any more children.

I had lived with my parents for nearly a year after the divorce and I knew I needed to take the chance of living on my own. I searched for weeks when I finally found a place on the same side of the river from Chase. I knew this would be a good move and possibly my relationship with Chase would move to the next level. We talked about getting married and it might just happen, after all, I did pray for my Knight in Shining Armor to take me away.

Chase and I were inseparable by now and everyone figured we were already married since you didn't see him without me. This went on for months and then there was a major change between us. This was where communication was key, and I thought the key was misplaced because we were sitting still and not moving forward anymore. Chase started working in Terrebonne Parish for the Sheriff's Department and we started to spend less time together. I would bring him to work at times so we could be together, but things still seemed a little off between us. I started getting confused and I wasn't sure if it was the endometriosis, or maybe he didn't want to be with me anymore. I had begun thinking, as long as I was married he wanted me, but now I was divorced. I was just a passing thought like the song, "The Thrill is Gone". Too many things were happening, and I started to question if my opportunity of being happy would ever come. The pain overtook my thoughts to the point I stopped caring whether or not he stayed around.

My cycles had become so bad I was bleeding for months at a time and was going to the gynecologist weekly regarding the pain. My time with Chase diminished and I was actually okay with it. The thought of being in a great space with him was no longer a part of who I was. I just wanted to be by myself since I needed all my strength to care for my son. I then thought about it, my being in a great space was still there because I was no longer married to Ted and the pain I was experiencing felt like a walk in the park in comparison. I knew if the pain hadn't stopped I would have to consider having a hysterectomy. Maybe what Ted said was true and being damaged goods was the course for my life.

I continued to tell myself that it would get better and now I was divorced things would improve with Chase. Chase was an amazing man and would do just about anything for me, but I started to avoid him. I thought if I would avoid him he wouldn't want to have sex with me because the pain was unbearable. Months had passed, and Chase was always at work and I was happy knowing sex was the last thing on my mind. Part of me didn't want him and the other part of me wanted him to stay. I was so confused at times I didn't even want to be around me, but the one lasting thing that kept coming back to mind was this space was way better than being in an abusive relationship. This had turned out to be a very long year and the pain only made things worse. After the divorce, my mother had a stroke and, as always, I did my best to be there for her despite what happened in the past.

I didn't want Ted to come to the house anymore, so I would meet him in different spots, so he could get TJ for the weekends. Weeks went on and I decided to meet Ted in the parking lot off Franklin Ave since it was in an open area. We had begun to argue that night and I was assaulted by Ted in front of TJ. After the incident the Harbor police showed up first, handling the assault. The Harbor Officer told me, "You lucky I took the call because if NOPD would have taken it, you would be going to jail right now." I thanked him for showing up first because I didn't need this, especially after my mother's stroke. Later that night I told Chase and he suggested I should get a temporary restraining order to at least keep Ted away for a little while. A few days later, I got a peace bond since I wasn't sure if any of it would work. Maybe being in a great space was something of a passing thought which was destined to never happen. Would I ever be in such a space? This was the ongoing question I would ask myself daily.

My pain only got worse and I found myself back at the gynecologist almost daily. After passing out I had made it up in my mind I couldn't take the pain and had to make a choice.

The more pain I was in the less time I wanted to spend with Chase. I thought if I told him how I was feeling then he wouldn't want to be with me and I would fall into the category of "damaged goods".

I informed my doctor how I couldn't take the pain anymore and something needed to be done because I couldn't continue suffering. The gynecologist did all he could, and after several months of fighting I had the hysterectomy. I found the nerve to tell Chase and then it hit me that the great space had never left, and I chose not to go in the direction for comfort. Sometimes we block blessings and do not even realize it. I continued to do this daily. I figured I had an opportunity to get off the roller coaster after being on it for so long, but I decided to stay on for another ride. I had reached the end of the tunnel and I could see light and things started looking up and again I chose to go in the other direction.

After weeks of preparation, it was time for surgery and having a hysterectomy was the next best thing to winning the lottery. Since I never won, being pain free would have to do. Hopefully Chase and I would get back on track and that wonderful life I was waiting for would be within reaching distance. I mean, how could I endure all of this pain and still be in my right mind. It was the constant question being asked and now I finally had an answer.

The day before the surgery I had to do the necessary preparation and never expected I would prepare myself for another journey. The day I completed my blood work for the surgery I met a man who played another role in my life causing me to question who I was again. Terrin was the phlebotomist who completed all the blood work. I was always oblivious to what was going on around me and he asked several questions trying to find out if I was married or even dating someone. My only concern at the time was getting everything finished so I could have my surgery and to restart my life with Chase.

Terrin would ask subtle questions and I entertained it for a little while before giving him my number before I left. I didn't think anything of it since I was only focusing on the surgery. Chase continued to show so much affection I felt bad about how I was treating him after the divorce. I realized he was only reacting to my behavior causing him to keep his distance. Chase did his best to show me he loved me and all I was focused on was stopping the pain, so I could enjoy my life. The countdown has begun, and I was never more excited about anything else like having surgery. The great space was closer, and I could even taste it and it tasted good.

It was surgery day. You would have thought it was my birthday. I was so excited. I was happy, but my mother was indifferent since it was their anniversary. December 11, 2001 was the date my prayers were answered, the day I would no longer be in pain, but once again I would prepare to get back on the roller coaster for another ride. The surgery went well, and I was feeling like a new person. When I finally woke up after surgery I was in pain but for a different reason. My mother asked me, "Who was that guy who showed up?" I didn't have a clue of who she was talking about and I wanted to rest so I could start walking around. This was the only way I could leave the hospital and my intended plan.

Later Chase had come to the hospital and he did something completely amazing. He showed up with some flowers and a card. I thought it was sweet, especially after all I had done over the past few months. When I read the card, it had a blank check and it read "Cash" at the bank of his heart. He made me smile and things started to seem real and the "great space" was at the front door ready for me to come in. Visiting hours were over and Chase was told by the nurse he needed to leave for the night and to come back in the morning. Chase finally made his way back to the room and spent the night. He crawled in the bed next to me and told me, "I know one of the nurses and she said I could stay." My knight had shown up, but he couldn't ride me off just yet since I was confined to a hospital bed. When I woke up in the morning Chase was gone, but the smile in my heart never left.

Around noon Terrin showed up and asked, "Did your mother tell you I stopped by?" I told him "Yes, but didn't realize you were who she was talking about." Terrin stayed for only an hour since he was on his lunch break. I started to debate if I should take a chance. I was trying to get things back on track with Chase. I told Terrin I was glad he stopped by and he asked if he could call me sometimes. I agreed and then he left. I was flattered but I loved Chase and wanted to make things work between us.

Chase and I did great for a few months and things went back to the way they were. I couldn't blame my endometriosis anymore. I knew the relationship had gone south and maybe it was time to move on. I started talking to Terrin more and made up my mind that maybe I should call it quits with Chase. After all, we dated for over five years and it might be time for something or someone new.

I called Chase the next morning and told him the relationship was over, and he couldn't understand why. I told him it wasn't working anymore, and I wished him the best. It must have hit him hard because later I got a call from his best friend, Damien, who stated, "Chase truly loves you. Is there any way to work things out between the two of you?" I told him, "Damien, you didn't need to call for Chase because there is nothing that will change my mind." I loved Chase, but I didn't believe he loved me anymore and I felt that my "Knight" had left on the horse without me. I figured with Terrin coming into the picture I could give him a chance. All my other relationships in the past were terrible, so who's to say what could happen.

13

ALL FOR NOTHING

Terrin and I started dating immediately and I did all I could to get my mind off Chase. For the first few months it felt like a dream because Terrin made me the center of his world. I was excited to have someone look at me like nothing else mattered. Maybe I was looking at this all wrong and Terrin could have made everything different for me. I didn't have anything to lose since I had already been married and had my son. Terrin was also married before so I thought he would understand what I've been through, or at least I thought.

Terrin had three children and had been divorced. I was grateful he was understanding about me not being able to have any more children. This made the relationship somewhat more bearable. As the relationship continued, I figured giving him a chance would make me feel good about myself after all I went through with Ted. With Terrin in the picture, Ted had no choice but to leave me alone and my life could start to turn around.

Over time things started to get worse with Ted again as he had become obsessed with harassing me. Ted would show up at the house and would leave threatening messages on the phone, so I had to decide what to do next.

I was tired of Ted's behavior and allowed Terrin to move in with me. I wasn't big on doing it and I definitely wasn't raised that way, but I figured with Terrin at the house Ted would leave me alone knowing someone else was living there. Terrin moved in and I wasn't sure if I had made the right decision.

The first few months were great for me. I didn't hear from Ted, and Terrin proved to be a wonderful person. I started to believe I might have the chance to be happy and maybe Terrin could be the one. I didn't know why I was so set on finding "the one", but at this point in my life I just wanted to be happy. I enjoyed how our relationship was going then everything seemed to fall apart. I started to regret I allowed Terrin to move in and now I needed to find a way to get him out the house.

I had come home from work to find Terrin laying on the sofa and the house was a mess. I questioned him, "Why is the house still a mess?" The answer I got was frustrating, causing me to tell him to get out of the house. I was so angry I yelled at him and told him he needed to get out at that very moment. I didn't care where he went, but I needed him to get out of my house. From that moment our relationship changed forever. I wanted to be happy and more and more I realized I didn't know what happiness was. How can I experience something I had no clue about?

I decided I needed a change and looked for somewhere to move. I moved back to Jefferson parish hoping things would start to get better for me and TJ. The move was complete, and life was good until there was a small twist in the plan. I found out Terrin moved into an apartment complex down the street from me. I didn't know how to feel, I mean of all the places to move, and I moved near Terrin. A month had passed and Terrin decided to make his presence known and explained why he decided to move down the street from me and of course, his explanation was interesting.

I decided to meet with Terrin to hear what he had to say. He explained he didn't want the relationship to end, but it was necessary since he had a lot going on. When I initially met Terrin he was living on his own, but it wasn't the best of neighborhoods and moving in with me was a step up for him. He explained he couldn't keep up with me and figured I wouldn't understand so he tried to piss me off intentionally. Terrin's family lived in a well-known housing project and he did all he could to detach himself from them, and being with me gave him the opportunity he was looking for. I didn't believe what he said and maybe I was being difficult, but I knew his explanation would be interesting. He must have thought I was going to believe his story and pick up where we left off. Only in his dreams.

We decided we would just be friends. After all, I needed to get myself together too. I found out later he started dating someone else and he never told me the truth, which only made things worse between us. We would still hang out from time to time, but not the way we did when we were dating. As time passed, I learned his intention to be with me wasn't right, and I was just another person he was trying to get over on.

This was the hardest time for me. I developed habits I wasn't proud of, but those habits molded me in a way I would have never imagined. I started drinking heavily and having sex with any and everybody because I didn't care about myself. I admit I had become a functional alcoholic, but I still did my best to care for my son. I hoped my actions wouldn't affect TJ, and by God's grace it didn't. I understand it now, but I didn't back then.

I started working for a well-renowned social services agency and I did my best to make sure my drinking wouldn't get in the way. My favorite drink was apple martinis; vodka was my weakness. I had developed a routine no one knew of, but eventually my drinking allowed those around me to know there was a problem. I would drink like a fish and eventually I had to go to the doctor because my drinking decided to show me who was boss.

I was upset by what took place between me and Terrin, and before I knew it I was dealing with seven different men. I made it up my mind I would get a tattoo hoping that would make a change in my life. Even though my life was spiraling out of control, I still did what it took to be there for TJ and I wasn't going to expose him to anything else. TJ was only 9 years old, and he was still working through the fact his father wasn't around. I wasn't sure why I was spiraling out of control, but I figured some love was better than no love at all. I never understood why I was so unlucky with love, and I would do whatever I could to not feel so lonely or unwanted.

I was still working at the mental health agency and got really sick at work. I went to the doctor to find out I was being referred to a urologist. I didn't think anything of it until I was told I was having complications with my kidneys and bladder and needed to have a stint put in from the damage. I had to wrap my mind around this because I knew I did it to myself and it wasn't fair to TJ. I had the procedure done and made up my mind I wasn't going to drink anymore.

Things didn't go well with the procedure. I only lasted three weeks with the stint before I had to have it removed. It was supposed to be in for at least six months, and it was apparent I wasn't going to make it. I went back to the doctor and the words said changed my mindset about drinking and I decided to stop. I had to make sure nothing happened to TJ even if that something was me. TJ was still upset by the divorce and he didn't need to have his mother disappoint him too. My son was my life line, and I decided to do things differently and not think of myself. It was all or nothing, and ALL was the better choice, since NOTHING had been around for a long time and it was time for NOTHING to leave.

My demeanor changed and I started doing things completely different. I left all the men alone and stopped drinking. I wanted to be the best mother I thought I knew how to be, and make TJ my focus in my life. To make the change permanent, I decided I needed to buy a house, but first I needed to get my finances in order. Weeks earlier I had found out that I had an opportunity to participate in a pilot program working with infants which offered more money. So of course, I applied and got the job. This was the first time I heard from God and knew what was said to me, that man couldn't change or stop the process.

After my divorce, I had to file for bankruptcy so buying a house was definitely out of the question, but God showed me that wasn't the case. I never knew this was the start of what I had asked God to do. Remember I told God, "If you get me out of this, then Lord I will do whatever you want." I had my mind made up I wasn't going to pay rent anymore and the door was now opened to getting a house. It was November of 2003 and my bankruptcy was filed in October 2002. Thinking about buying a house should have been the last thing on my mind, but God showed me otherwise and the process started to home ownership.

14

NEW PAGE SAME STORY

The hunt was on to find a house. I started looking in January of 2004 and I decided to move back across the river again in the same city of Gretna. I know it seemed crazy, especially after all the hell Ted put me through after the divorce. The search was funny and stressful at the same time and lasted for three months. I joked about the search since all the houses had 13 in the address and I informed my agent it was definitely not going to work for me. I finally found the house and yes it didn't have the number 13 in the address.

I decided not to date anybody and after my bout with the stint incident, I knew I needed a break. My only focus was getting the house and myself together. Everything else would fall into place and the "great space" was buying a house and not being in a relationship. Those few months were pleasant and drama free for once in my life. Maybe caring for my son was what I was supposed to do, and a relationship was far out of reach for me.

The time had come, and the purchase of the house was complete. I was now a homeowner living in a small incorporated town across the river. Ironically enough, the house wasn't too far from the one rented when I first moved to Gretna. The day I signed the paperwork it felt like I was making the biggest mistake of my life and there were so many pages to sign. My mother had come with me, but I still felt this was too much to handle. Once the process was over, I was able to breathe knowing this had to be the space needed to start my life over again. After the closing we went to lunch to celebrate, but my stomach had another agenda.

I literally got sick at the table wondering if I did the right thing.

I always had something going on with me and the move posed to be one of those things. The house needed a few changes, so I decided to paint my bedroom. I got to Home Depot and the guy behind the counter went out of his way to help me find the color that I wanted.

We talked the entire time and he made sure I had the right shade of purple for my bedroom. Before I knew it, I gave him my number before I left the store. His name was Brent and he was discharged from the Marines, but he refused to tell me why. I didn't care for Marines, but Brent made sure those negative thoughts would stay in place.

Brent and I dated briefly, and it was okay because I wasn't looking for a relationship anyway. In the beginning, Brent's strange behavior would happen a lot, but I ignored it because he was an ex-Marine. I figured his behavior was one of the reasons why he was discharged.

Brent would always be at the house and I started to question if he was still working at Home Depot. One morning Brent asked me to call the store and make up a reason why he couldn't come to work. I guess I didn't want to notice, but the relationship started to get crazy.

Brent started talking about moving in and I refused to answer him. I eventually told him I wasn't moving in with another man unless he was my husband. The more I ignored him the more he continued to talk about making plans for us long term. I wasn't looking for anything serious and was not moving anyone into a house I worked so hard to get. It was time to move in and the strangest thing happened which was never explained. The day I finished painting my bedroom I decided to sleep in the back bedroom because the paint was extremely strong. My mattress was under the window, but I didn't mind because I was tired and needed some rest, so I wouldn't wake up with a headache. I got up to go to the bathroom and then laid back down. A few minutes later I heard a noise and I wasn't sure if I was dreaming or hearing things, but the window shattered over my head. I immediately called 911 and waited for them to get there. My next thought was to call Brent, but he didn't answer his phone and I thought it was strange.

Once the police got there it was like Mayberry from the Andy Griffin Show. There were five police cars and the canine unit. In my mind I thought "was this all necessary for a broken window?". I continued to call Brent, but he never answered the phone and now I was pissed. All I could think about was he had something to do with it since I told him earlier he wasn't moving in with me. The police indicated they couldn't determine who broke the window and the fuse from the air conditioner was the item used and it was missing. The police officer also stated, "We will take the screwdriver to determine if they could pull prints." The funny part was the officer took the screwdriver and put it in his back pocket without a glove. I knew then I was living in Mayberry for sure and would never find out what actually happened to the window.

The next morning, I did something I shouldn't have, but it was the only alternative. I called Ted and asked him to install an alarm in the house. Ted owned his own alarm company with one of his friends. I only called him since he hadn't done anything else for me and TJ over the years and this was the least he could do for me. Ted had come later to install the alarm and I didn't need him to be there while my father was there having the window repaired. All day I was calling Brent and he finally showed up that night.

The alarm was in and Ted even agreed to take TJ for the night to give me a break. Brent stated, "I must be having problems with my phone and I just got your message." I just looked at him and I knew he had something to do with the window, but I couldn't prove it. Brent looked at me and stated, "I told you that I needed to move in and if I did this wouldn't happen." I told him, "Please get out of my house; I don't want to see you anymore." I got my confirmation and knew it was him. Being an ex-Marine, he knew what to do not leave any proof. He was the one who broke the window.

It was never a dull moment and only a few months had passed before Terrin popped back up. With the alarm in, I knew Brent would stay away, but Terrin was a different story. He heard I moved and figured he could come back. I entertained Terrin and we went out a few times, but I made it clear to him it would be on my terms. Things were fine between us when another twist happened. I found out I got the position with the state and Terrin decided he wanted to marry me. I told Terrin, "We're not playing these games, and if we get married it's not going to be all this back and forth." He agreed and in a matter of a month, we got married in May of 2005.

Honestly, I didn't want to marry Terrin, but I figured what the hell since my track record wasn't the best and I knew it would keep Ted away for sure. We woke the morning of May 16th which was a Monday and off we went to get married. It wasn't anything special and it was like going to the store. We got to the judge's chambers and didn't even have witnesses. The judge and his secretary signed the marriage license, which didn't make the day special at all. Once it was over, we went to lunch and back home. Here we go again with a new start and the start wasn't going great at all. I settled and hoped things would get better since I was like oil and men were water.

My marriage to Terrin went great for the first few weeks and then things started to sour. It was only a month and I knew I married the wrong man again. I went in knowing I needed to walk away, but it was a long road before it was determined I could leave. I should have talked to God first, but I had talked to everyone but Him. It was for God to let me know and I couldn't make a move a moment too soon.

15

ANSWERING ANOTHER CALL

Terrin and I had been married for three months when Hurricane Katrina hit the city in August of 2005. I remembered it like yesterday because my mother called me up and said, "Either yo ass is coming with us, or yo ass is on yo own because we are leaving and going to Houston." I turned on the television and called Terrin to tell him I was taking TJ and we were going with my parents. Terrin was okay with the idea and shared he would stay in the city since he needed to work. I packed some clothes for me and TJ and left with my parents since no one in the city knew what to expect if Katrina was going to directly hit the city.

Houston was the normal destination since my sister Kristen lived there for a while. We all thought it would only be for a few days and then go back home. The storm did pass, but the city didn't fare well and we weren't able to go back for months. Before the storm I tried my best to get Terrin out of the city, but everything was shut down and it took a while for him to get to Houston. The entire time I was worried. We were just married, and I didn't need to be a widow after being married for three months. My mind was everywhere, and I wasn't going to stop until he was in Houston with me and

I knew he was safe. It was the longest weekend ever and I worried thinking I was going to be by myself. It wasn't the best marriage, but at least I had somebody, and people wouldn't think something was wrong with me.

Terrin finally made it to Houston so I was happy knowing he was there and things started to change. We found out we couldn't go back to the city and had to make a decision. We decided we would stay in Houston, but first we needed to move from near my sister. Looking for an apartment wasn't easy and we ended up by his best friend's apartment instead. During the transition, it was confirmed FEMA would give out money to cover expenses while we were there, but only for a few months. After I shared the news, Terrin started to act strange then said the weirdest thing to make me think I made a mistake in marrying him. Terrin stated, "I know that you are going to give me half of the money when we get it right?" This was weird and I wondered why he would even say that in the first place. Once the money hit my account Terrin immediately asked if he could go shopping. I was focused on trying to figure out what we were going to do next and all he wanted to do was shop. I was angry, but we did need some clothes since we only packed for three days and weren't sure how long we would be in Houston. I realized I had a bad taste in my mouth and was trying to figure out how I was going to get rid of it as well as how I would end the relationship.

It was September and time for school. I was able to get TJ in school trying my best to give him a life of normalcy, whatever that was. We stayed in Houston from August to October and it felt like the longest time of my life, not knowing if I would make it to the end of the year being married a second time. I did my best to avoid Terrin and put all my attention into finding somewhere to live and making sure TJ was not affected by this new change. This routine went on for several weeks and we were told we could go back home, but to what? I made up my mind that I was going home, especially after my job told me I had to be back at work by the 3rd of October.

We decided to go back to New Orleans, not knowing what to expect once we got back. I was hoping the city wouldn't be too messed up and if it was, then we would come back to Houston and I would look for another job. We were informed by the news that we had to show proof to get back in the city and Terrin never changed his address. To avoid the possibility of being questioned we took another route to get back into the city. Remember I didn't live in New Orleans, but on the outskirts of Jefferson parish which was across the Mississippi River. New Orleans took the direct hit and Gretna supposedly was fine, so getting home wasn't blocked off. We made it back in the city and it was ire. It was absolutely quiet, and the only noise was from the helicopters which were flying over the city nonstop. It was desolate, and I was in disbelief that my home, my city was destroyed and now it was time to rebuild and start over.

When we went to the house, Terrin went in first while me and TJ stayed in the truck. When he came back out I knew it must have been a mess. Terrin surprised me and stated, "The house is fine, and the biggest problem is the refrigerator." I needed to throw it out because of the maggots. I was grateful, but I was now worried about what my parents' house looked like and if I would be able to get to it. I was now plotting how I was going to get there to check out the damage.

TJ was turning eleven and we celebrated his birthday twice that year. I chose to do it in order to take his mind off all the chaos going on. I felt like I was trapped and asked God why all this was happening. By then I was just putting up with Terrin and doing my best to get my parents and my sister back in the city. I figured if I focused on my family I could block Terrin out and not think about the mistake I had made again. A few weeks later my family was back in the city. I waited to see their house and when we made it the house was destroyed far beyond what words could describe.

The neighborhoods were destroyed as we drove down the street and it was evident by the water lines to all the houses in the area. There wasn't any activity in the city and we all were in disbelief once we made it to their house. Once we made it there no one moved and just sat in the car. I was glad TJ wasn't there to see the house. He was with Ted because Ted's family had been back in the city for a while. My father finally got out of the car and went into the house. I decided to stay outside in the car with my mother since I didn't need her to have a meltdown right away. We continued to converse until we heard my father open the garage door. When my father came to the car, he told us to put on our face masks because the smell of mold was strong. If we had to put on masks, then what we were going to see must have been bad.

After putting on the face masks we went into the house and once my mother saw the house destroyed, she broke down and started to cry. In my mind, I was wondering why this happened to them and not me. I just bought my house a year ago and they had been in their house for nearly fifteen years. As we walked through the house everything my parents ever had was destroyed, and there was nothing anyone could do about it. We finally made it to the garage and noticed both my car and my mother's car were full of mold. I was actually amazed by the colors of mold and was curious to examine it. My father told me, "Leave it alone so you won't get sick." From that moment on, my life and my parents' life would never be the same.

I made up my mind immediately that my parents were going to stay with me, but I needed to talk to Terrin first. He was my husband and it was what I was supposed to do, right? I spoke to Terrin and we agreed that my parents and my sister would stay with us until they were able to get things back on track. Hopefully it wouldn't take long, and life would get back to normal.

My life has always had twists and turns but letting my parents move in was something I wasn't prepared for. It's true, the statement, "You can't have two women in the same house", and it posed to be true with me and my mother. Things continued to go south between us and it went from being my house to hers. My mother made changes which suited her and disregarded the fact that it belonged to me. Daily my mother would do things she felt were needed, and most of the time she never asked me or Terrin how we felt about what she did.

My mother started to show paranoid tendencies and would make changes nearly every week. I came home one day after work and I noticed the kitchen window was frosted. I asked, "Mom why did you do this?" and my mother stated, "I did it because people could see in and I didn't need that." I looked at her and went into my room because the window was up high and if someone got up there, they would have been seen. Terrin would stay late at work, so I stayed in my room from the moment I walked in the house. The next morning Terrin asked, "What happened to the kitchen window?" I explained to him what my mother said and all he did was laugh and told me he was going by his mother's house and would be home late. I already had an awful relationship with him, and having my parents living there only made things worse.

A few weeks had passed, and I would come home to more craziness and would go to my room so I didn't have to deal with either of them. Our cars were destroyed, and we purchased new cars on the same day. My mother went back to work, but she was required to commute back and forth to Baton Rouge. Things were calm for a while between us and there weren't any problems at the house. Terrin continued to spend more time with his mother and I spent more time in my room. I questioned what was going on around me and why it had gotten to this point in my life.

My mother was constantly going back and forth to work and decided to get a rental car to make the trip. It's an hour commute and about 70 miles both ways, so my mother got the rental to eliminate the miles on her car. One evening I made it home and went straight to my room and my mother called me into the kitchen. My mother said, "I need you to move your car on the street so I could put the rental in its place." I immediately lost it and told her "I'm not moving my car and it doesn't make sense why you are spending money on a rental when you have a new car just sitting in the driveway already." I walked off and went back to my room. I was angry and knew they had to get out of the house and the next day I spoke to my father and told him how I felt. My father surprised me and confirmed they needed to leave. My father said, "You know how your mother is, and to keep the peace you just need to let her do what she wants." I went off and told my father, "Y'all have to get out because this ain't gonna work anymore! My house has been turned upside down and all you can say is let her have her way." I left the room and went back into my room and called my Aunt Shayna to let her know how I was feeling and about what happened with her sister. I felt trapped because nobody was on my side and everyone was agreeing with the things my mother was doing.

Several days had passed and my father said, "I talked to your mother and we are going to move to Baton Rouge to make it easier for her and work." I just stood there not showing any emotions, but deep down I was excited they were finally moving out of the house. Not saying it would fix my relationship with Terrin, but now I didn't have to deal with my mother trying to be in control of the entire house anymore.

My parents finally moved out. My mother didn't speak to me for about five months and honestly, I was okay with it. I had my house back and now I was trying to figure out what I needed to do with my marriage. Terrin was working more and it didn't bother me because I was doing my best to focus on my job and taking care of my son. It got to the point Terrin would only speak when it was necessary, and he mentioned that his son was coming to live with us. I just got my house back and now his son was moving in. This constant roller coaster ride was making me sick to my stomach and I was ready to get off for good.

It was 2006 and the year was more interesting than I cared to mention. Tyson moved in and I asked Terrin, "Please explain to me again why Tyson is moving in?" Terrin stated, "Rochelle is making him live with us because if he doesn't, then her boyfriend won't marry her." I had to wrap my mind around this. Terrin just told me his ex-wife was getting rid of her son because her boyfriend told her that if she didn't he wasn't going to marry her. I knew my life was messed up, but that was definitely something on another level for me to deal with. I was at least trying to hold true to my vows "for better or worse", not realizing the worst had already taken place with his son moving in. It was a trying year and I found myself praying more than ever to get some answers on what to do since none of this was making sense.

Tyson was living with us and it was a constant battle because Terrin showed more favoritism to his children and treated TJ like he was the problem. Rochelle also had become a problem thinking she could dominate what took place in my house. Terrin's children would do whatever they wanted at the house and Terrin refused to correct them. Terrin had two daughters, Kiki and Shelly. These two were unique in who they were, but Tyson gave them a run for their money. Rochelle figured she could come in, tell me how to raise her children and I wouldn't have a problem. I made up my mind, I wasn't letting anyone run over me in my house.

As time passed, Tyson did all he could to go back to his mother, but being the person who hated defeat, I was going to do all I could to raise him, but it backfired in my face. The more I tried to make Tyson feel at home, the more he destroyed my house in order to get back to his mother and sisters. Tyson figured in his little mind he could get put out and then he'd have no choice but to go back to his mother's house. I tried, but this deed had become too much for me, and I had reached my limit not only with Terrin, but with his children too. This went on for months and I had enough, so it was time for Tyson to go back to his mother for good.

I survived the entire year with Terrin and his son, but it was now time for me to switch gears and answer another call. It was a new year and I was hoping 2007 would be a better start to my life. First Katrina, my parents and then Tyson living with us had me question, "What else could happen?" Well I guess I asked the question way too soon. I was preparing for another journey and this one was not what I was prepared for. I forgot what I had promised God, but He didn't forget and now the call was about to start. Terrin and I were still at the same point, but now we were not having sex and the truth of the matter was, I didn't care and hoped he would come home and say he didn't want to be with me anymore.

It was a Sunday morning and I was still in bed and I felt a tap on my shoulder causing me to flinch. I noticed Terrin was actually in the bed for once, so I laid back down. A few minutes later I felt a tap on my shoulder again. This time I told Terrin, "Will you please stop touching me?" Terrin looked at me and said, "I didn't touch you so leave me alone." Of course, me being me said, "I'm not surprised because you haven't touched me in a while anyway." I turned my head and laid back on the pillow. Not realizing what was going on I heard "You need to go to church, it's time." Now I knew that wasn't Terrin and figured I was just hearing things so I got up. I eventually got dressed and left the house. I just drove around because I didn't have a clue where I was going, but I knew I needed to find a church home.

For weeks, I visited several churches, but none of them felt right until it happened, and it was confirmed I needed to be at this one particular church. I was driving down the street and saw a billboard of a well-renowned pastor and it was as if my eyes were fixated and I couldn't stop staring. The cars behind me started blowing because I had stopped traffic. I knew this was where I needed to be, so I decided the next week to check the church out.

I went to the church and I was actually excited to go. When I got there, I didn't realize it was the end of the service. I was a little disappointed, but I was told the next service would start in 30 minutes and I was welcome to stay. I felt like a deer caught in headlights because I wasn't trying to leave, but didn't know what to do. I stayed for the next service and found myself joining the same day. I guess from that point on I answered the call and couldn't wait to find out where this journey was going to take me.

I found out the following week the pastor was the head of two different churches, but I had become a member of the second church. It felt good to be a part of something, and having people who actually wanted to be around me. I continued to go for several weeks and this was the "great space" I was looking for and for once I didn't want it to end. I looked forward to going, but Terrin refused to go and I was fine with his decision. It even got to the point Terrin was telling people I was caught up with the church and he didn't want to be caught up with all that church stuff. Being at church was my peace, and yes, being a part of something made me feel good about myself. I actually started to see myself in a different way and not the damaged goods I was told I was for a long time.

A few weeks went by and I attended a new members meeting at the church. As I was sitting in the meeting I noticed Miller, and I started to smile. After the meeting I went up to Miller to jog his memory about who I was. When TJ was one year old I worked with Miller at a famous restaurant which was located at the temporary casino in downtown New Orleans. Once we were caught up I explained to Miller that I was married again. The funniest thing happened. Miller stated," I'm not worried, you won't be married to him long." I didn't know what to say and just laughed it off. I hugged Miller and told him I never thought I would see him again after all this time and I knew I was at the right church because I was reunited with a longtime friend.

I started spending more time at church, and Terrin started spending more time elsewhere. I got into every ministry I could think of because being connected to other people felt good and I made sure TJ was a part of all that the church had to offer. Ted wasn't around much so I wanted to make sure TJ had enough exposure to show him it was okay his father wasn't around. Life was great now and I was glad to tell every one of my new-found love, and the best part was I knew I could be loved by my church family without any strings attached.

For a period of ten months my life seemed to be falling into place. Being at church allowed me to embrace all the things that had taken place in my life, and God showed me I didn't do anything wrong to cause all the hell I went through. I always joked and said, "God does have a sense of humor, especially when it comes to my life." The funny part is that God was always in control and when He's ready for you, it is definitely without warning and on His time. The church had a ceremony for a group of ministers who were being ordained as elders at the church. I decided to go to the ceremony, and was excited to see them being elevated, but this was when I officially answered the call on my life. As I'm writing this I heard the Holy Spirit say, "This is what I have for you." I remember saying, "I'm not doing this," and the person sitting next to me said, "What did you say?" I immediately said, "Nothing," and that's when the journey started.

This was when I knew, at that moment, God chose me, and I couldn't tell him "No" so I spoke to my pastor about my decision to become a minister. I remember it like it was yesterday when I met with my pastor to share what the Holy Spirit had shared. My pastor said, "I give both my blessing and my condolences. This journey will be the best experience of your life, but you will lose a lot of people along the way." I didn't understand it right away, but as time continued I realized exactly what my pastor said was true. About five months later I had begun studying to become a minister and yes, I started losing friends left and right. Terrin was one of them. I was now considered a Minister-In-Training (MIT) and it lasted for a period of 18 months, but God showed me a completely different view and it was extremely beautiful from where I was.

I had an idea Terrin was seeing someone else, but I just couldn't put my finger on it especially when I was studying to be a minister. Everyone would tell me Terrin was messing around, but I would say, "I can't leave until God tells me to do so." This went on for months until I decided to check the phone bill. The bill had come in the mail and that night I started to highlight the one number that would show up constantly. By the time I finished highlighting, the pages were nearly all yellow except for one or two lines which showed my number. The calls would last over 20 minutes and then my number would show less than a minute. I found myself getting angry because the calls would start the moment I left the house and lasted until he decided to come home at night. I thought I needed to confront him, but I left it alone until Terrin did something that made me mad. Terrin had come home early one night and was on the phone. I was curious about who he was on the phone with so I asked him. He only said, "Shelly". Then I said, "Tell Shelly I say Hi." Terrin ignored me and didn't say anything and sat on the sofa at the other end. This went on for weeks and I thought something was truly wrong with his daughter, not realizing he was talking to the woman he was seeing on the side. When I realized what was going on I knew I had to do something and do it quickly.

It was our third anniversary and Terrin decided he would work the weekend. I said, "Why do you need to work; ask your boss if you could have the weekend off since it's our anniversary?" Terrin looked at me and said, "I can't get out of it and I have to go to Lake Charles since it's my turn to go out of town." He was a phlebotomist, so I didn't think anything of it, but I knew something wasn't right about what he said to me. Terrin left for the weekend and I ended up being by myself. What a wonderful way to spend our anniversary.

While he was on the road, Terrin called and said, "Since my computer stopped working could you transfer some money, so I could get another one when I get to Lake Charles." Still not thinking anything of what was going on, I transferred the money without hesitation.

The following month I was going to Birmingham for a church conference for three days. I thought if I left for a few days I could clear my head and maybe things would get better, at least on my end. The closer it got to leaving the more Terrin would spend time away from the house. I needed to find out for myself and maybe if I talked to her I would get some closure when making my move. I knew I couldn't call her from the house or when Terrin was around, so I decided to call from work. I called on a Friday from my office phone and was curious to see if she would call back. The entire weekend nothing was said and I was perfectly fine with it. As usual he wasn't home, so I just had to wait until I got back to work to see if I had received a returned call. Monday had come and I couldn't wait to get to work to check my messages. When I checked them, Shelly called seven times and I got the nerve up to call her back. When I called her, we had the most interesting conversation. Shelly said, "Terrin didn't tell me that he was married, and who are you supposed to be again?" I said, "I'm his wife and all those things that he told you about, it all belongs to me." The conversation with Shelly continued to be interesting especially when she told me she was married. I informed her I just needed to know so I could make my next move. Shelly said,"

Well he can't be with me since I have a husband and two kids, sorry."

After I finished my call with Shelly I called Terrin and told him, "I just got off the phone with Shelly." He asked, "Why are you calling my daughter?" I then said, "No I was on the phone with your boo, and she told me everything. I want you out by the time I come back from Birmingham." Terrin said, "Fine, because I was leaving anyway. And don't worry, I will be gone by the time you get back." That was the last conversation I had with him and I had my mind set on going to Birmingham.

It was time to leave for Birmingham and at the church conference I got confirmation I needed to get out of the relationship with Terrin. The speaking pastor mentioned, "some of you are going to the next level and you can't take certain people with you." All I remember was being on the floor and someone had to pick me up and I had to make a plan once I made it back to the city. God gave me exactly what I needed, and I was sticking to the plan. When God is ready for you to make a move, He will send all you need to make it happen quickly. The next morning, I left Birmingham and felt great about the next journey in my life.

I made it home, but Terrin never moved out so I immediately called my father to change the locks. While my father was changing the locks, I decided to leave and got rid of my wedding ring. I worked at a jewelry store and knew I wouldn't have any problems getting something new. I figured I didn't need it anymore and this was my way to start my new life with a shiny new ring. Terrin was put out on June 28th, and on July 7th I filed for divorce. I made up my mind that I wanted to be in my "great space" and maybe I had to do it with God's help this time. It was time to have a second chance at life, but it was only another journey I wasn't prepared for or at least I thought I wasn't.

16

A SECOND CHANCE AT LIFE

There was Danny and yes, he was just a friend. And no, I'm trying to sound like Biz Markie in no way. (For those who remember Biz Markie, you would understand what I'm saying, but if not, he's a rapper with his famous song "You Say He's Just a Friend.") I was working at criminal court by then and Danny worked as a Sheriff. I would run into him all the time when I had to go to the courthouse. We had become good friends and he was there when I decided to put Terrin out. Danny did all he could to cheer me up, but I wasn't feeling it. Danny went out of his way, but my feelings were not the same. We would talk on the phone for hours and I would share the things Terrin had done and he made a statement one day which messed my head up. He stated, "If it was me I would have never treated you that way and would always make sure that you were happy." I didn't know what to say because I only saw him as a friend. Now I'm sharing this for a reason because Danny will pop back up again.

I was getting adjusted to being on my own again and my goal was to make sure TJ was still okay too. I really didn't like working for the criminal court, but it paid the bills. The hardest part of the job was only getting paid once a month. This made me hate working even more, but I had to do it. I was assigned to two judges which made my job interesting. I worked for two female judges and one was the youngest African American female judge in the state. I was impressed by her accolades and spent a lot of my time in her courtroom just to see how she operated. I wasn't getting paid the best, but watching her work made the time there worthwhile.

One day I was in the courtroom and an officer walked in. This officer caught my attention, but we didn't talk to each other and only made eye contact. After seeing him that one time made me find reasons to stay in the courtroom hoping I would see him again. A few months later I was told he asked about me, but when he found out I was married I didn't see him anymore. I'm mentioning this too since he will also pop up later.

I was still getting adjusted to being on my own, but I knew it would take time and I would be alright. I jumped into my job so I wouldn't think about being alone or having to raise my son by myself. Months went by and things had become boring. In a sense, I felt like I was stuck. I wanted a job but felt like my heart wasn't in it at all. I finally met someone who I should have never started dating in the first place. This person had come at the wrong time and I attached myself to him for all the wrong reasons. His name was Jay and he was the true definition of a "Bad Boy". Jay had a decent upbringing, but he chose to do drugs out of boredom. Jay was only a few years older than me, but he spent most of his life in and out of jail. I don't know if I was attracted to him because of his lifestyle or because I just needed to have someone in my life. This was a roller coaster ride on a completely different track and I chose to stay on.

Jay lived more than an hour away and I would always have to drive to him because he didn't have a car. I had to get another car since the separation and I went to my mother for help. I had to give up my car after I agreed to let Terrin keep the truck he got for his birthday. I didn't have a problem, but my mother did. I never understood why money was such an issue for her and when asking for help- it was like an act of Congress. I would go once a month to see Jay and the result would always be the same when I got there. And the result was very toxic. Jay was in and out of jail so much he had to live with his parents. Jay's mother loved me and she told me, "You need to just leave my son alone because he's never going to change." The social worker in me felt otherwise, and that's why I stuck around. Sometimes we need saving, and trying to save others makes us think we're actually doing something right. I was doing something, and it was making a big mess of my life. So, between TJ, work, and Jay this was how my life went for a few months. Honestly, I wasn't happy with work or with Jay, knowing things would never get better. I went as far as bringing Jay to church thinking that would change him and nothing worked, which only made me more frustrated in the end.

It was 2009 and time for the annual drug court conference and I was excited because it was in California. I decided to take TJ with me because we would get the opportunity to go to Disneyland. I figured with all that had been going on we needed a break. Also, I would be able to spend some time with my cousins and my uncle while we were there. I focused on California and couldn't wait to leave. I had to make a big decision, and it was whether I wanted Jay to come with us. Remember, he wasn't the best candidate, and because of his background I couldn't afford to lose my job since it was only me raising TJ. I made the decision and Jay remained home. I made the right choice for a later decision.

While I was gone I called Jay to ask him a question, and from that point on I knew we could no longer be together. I asked Jay, "So does Cocaine make you feel better than me?" The answer I got messed my head up completely. Jay said, "Honestly you don't do anything for me, and I would rather have the coke over you any day." That was hurtful, and I knew when I got back that the relationship had to end. I did as much as I could to change him and I started to think about what his mother had told me. I enjoyed

Disneyland and my family, but I was ready to get back home to end the relationship with Jay since it was obviously a waste of both of our time.

A few weeks later I told Jay we needed to end the relationship and he agreed. After the breakup, all I could do was call Danny on the phone. I knew he would answer, and he was the ear to listen and the shoulder to cry on. The second chance I was thinking about didn't turn out how I planned it, but I was glad to get off the roller coaster since all the wheels had fallen off and I didn't need to get hurt anymore. I started to question God again about why all of this was happening, and what had I done so wrong that I couldn't find a decent man to be with. So, I started to put all my time into preparing to be a minister. Maybe this was all I had time for besides taking care of my son. It wasn't what I wanted, but then again, I didn't know what I wanted or needed for that matter.

Things were quiet for a while and I had settled in with being single. I was at the courtroom and on a break, I decided to check my phone and noticed a request from Chase's brother on one of the social media sites. I was shocked and immediately accepted the request. I hadn't heard from Hudson since I ended my relationship with Chase and I knew it had to have been at least eight years. After I accepted his request, we started sending messages to catch up and then Hudson said, "You know, Chase had been looking for you and I will let him know that I found you." I actually got excited to know he was concerned about me. Hudson also said, "Is it okay if I give Chase your number? I know he would love to talk to you himself." I said, "Most definitely and I would love to hear from him as well." In my mind, I started to think what if I mess up and this could possibly be the chance I have to start over.

Chase called, and we talked about why the relationship ended as well as got caught up with missing time. I was glad he called since there were so many loose ends to tie up. It was good to hear from him, but there was just one thing, Chase was married still, but to a different woman. Chase said jokingly, "If you would have never left me I would be married to you and not for a third time." I had to think about what was said and yes, we would probably still be married to this day. We both agreed things were different now and we both had relationships with God so we couldn't jump into a relationship like we did before. We decided to remain friends and keep in contact with each other.

Hope you're ready for another loop on the roller coaster because this was one I wasn't prepared for either. Things started looking up at the job and Chase and I reconnected, which made things even better. A few months had passed and there was a change in management which turned out to be a change for the worse. It was announced department wide that a new supervisor started and her name was Lindsey. Lindsey didn't appear to know what was going on, but she was friends with one of the judges so that could have been why she got the job. Lindsey had come in barking orders and was determined to cause division among everybody. I could be a pill at times, but I was determined not to let anybody talk to me disrespectfully, especially after all I went through with Ted. Lindsey and I were like oil and water and everyone knew it.

Lindsey had her clique and I was not a part of it and honestly, I didn't care to be. Lindsey had only been there a few months and things really started to change. I was called into her office. Lindsey said, "I think we might have to reconsider some things, and you will be monitored regarding your caseload. I have my eye on you." If it sounded confusing, Lindsey meant none of my clients were going back to jail and this wasn't considered a part of the program's intent of recidivism. The drug court program was designed to keep clients out of jail and I was doing so, but I guess that's not what she wanted. Things continued to get crazy and even my relationship with the judge had changed. I got a call from the judge and she even questioned what

I was doing and sided with Lindsey. I didn't make a big deal of it and asked Jesus to help me through this since I didn't have a clue what was going on.

When you ask God for something in prayer, you have to be prepared for what the outcome is and not what you expected to be. I would pray constantly especially now I had developed a relationship with God. I was trying to figure out what to do and how to handle my situation at work, but I forgot the battle wasn't mine in the first place. God answered my prayer, but not in the manner I thought. It was March 12, 2010 and it was a Friday. I got to work that morning and made up my mind that I wasn't going to do anything. I played solitaire and was on social media for the entire day. I wasn't in the mood and kept my door closed so I wouldn't be bothered. I survived the entire day without being bothered and at 3:00pm I was called into Lindsey's office. Lindsey said, "I'm sorry to inform you, but we are separating from you and you need to go to the Judicial Administrator's office for termination." Remember, I told you I had been praying for a resolve to my problem and this was God's way of doing so. I went to the JA's office, received my termination letter and was escorted out of the building. I wasn't the only one terminated that day. Michelle had to be calmed down since she was making a scene. I made it to my car and left from the building's parking garage. I was at peace, but wasn't sure what was going to happen next. All I knew I was happy knowing I didn't have to deal with the drama anymore.

It was now August of 2010 and I had been out of work for five months when Aaron surfaced again. Aaron was the guy I dated after high school and he went away to school in Georgia. Aaron was still living in Atlanta but would still come home from time to time to check up on his parents. We decided to see each other since he was in town, so I decided to meet him at his parents' house. I made the decision since I wasn't working and I didn't want him to know the truth. I didn't want him to think I didn't live up to his expectations and going to his parents' house would eliminate that thought.

Once I got to the house, I realized it was good to see Aaron, especially after eighteen years.

I was amazed; he hadn't changed a bit. We were older and yes, we both had some extra pounds we could afford to get rid of. Aaron said, "You know you should have been my wife, right?" All I could do was sit there and look at him. He just made the statement out of the blue so I didn't know what to say. Aaron had begun telling me how much he missed me and when he found out I was married the first time it messed his world up. I was shocked because I never knew he felt that way about me. We continued to talk about our lives over the years and before I left we decided we would try dating again.

We planned for me to come to Atlanta for Labor Day, but I still didn't let Aaron know I wasn't working. With him being in Atlanta, it would give me the opportunity to keep my distance without him knowing I was trying to get by. It was a week before going to Atlanta I started having these strange dreams. I would wake up scared because of what was going on in the dream. The dream would be of someone being hit by a garbage truck and finding the phone to call for help. I would never see the face, but I would immediately start praying for whoever it was. What made it so strange, I had the same dream three nights in a row before I left for Atlanta. Of course, I was scared because I didn't need anything to happen while I was on the road and now I was unemployed. I already had to deal with my mother regarding having the car in her name.

It was Labor Day weekend and time for me to leave. Before I left I prayed I would get to Atlanta without any problems. I made it to Atlanta and Aaron had a huge house, but hardly any furniture. I asked, "Aaron, how long have you been living here?" Aaron said, "Oh about four years now I think." This made me question if this was really his house because the only rooms furnished were the den and his bedroom and the house had five bedrooms. Aaron stated, "I got the house so when my fam comes they don't have to go to a hotel." Again, in my mind I'm thinking where were they going to sleep without any furniture?

We had a great weekend and I didn't want to leave, but I had to since my goal was to find a job quickly so I wouldn't have to go to my mother anymore. I left Atlanta the morning of Labor Day and made it back home safely with God's grace. I was surprised the entire time I was in Atlanta I didn't have one dream and I was grateful. The same night I had the same dream again, causing me to question what was going on. The next morning was a regular day and the part time job I was working, at the time, was something to do which kept my mind off everything going on. It was now Wednesday and the day that my life changed forever.

I saw a few clients and once I was done I called the church and told Miller I would be on my way. My reason for going to the church was to prepare for a huge event. Our pastor's son was doing a revival and I was assisting with getting things together before he had come into town. The client I saw lived on the eastern side of the river from where the church was, and once I met with him and his mother I would jump on the bridge to head across the river. The appointment was over, and I set out for church. As I was crossing the river there was a red garbage truck that was beside me, but I didn't pay it any attention since I was focused on getting to the church. Danny just happened to call, and I had him on speaker while I was sitting at the red light. I looked up in my rearview mirror and saw the same garbage truck that just passed me on the bridge, but it appeared he wasn't stopping behind me. The dream I had was coming true so I braced myself for the impact.

The garbage truck slammed into the back of the car and pushed me into another garbage truck. The front windshield shattered as the car bounced off the other garbage truck. Everything seemed to be going in slow motion and I closed my eyes. I knew I was dead, and when I opened my eyes I reached for my phone and called Miller. I was screaming trying to tell him what happened because all I could think of was how to get out. Miller asked, "Where are you so I can get to you?" I couldn't really answer the question and said," I'm at the traffic circle." Miller knew exactly where I was and I got off the phone. I started to panic because I figured the car would catch on fire and I needed to get out quickly, but I couldn't because the seatbelt was stuck. I immediately started praying asking God to get me out of this because I didn't know what to do.

A lady walked up to the car and said, "Sweetie calm down. My husband checked, and the car isn't leaking any fluid, and we are going to help you get out." I stated, "I just need to get out because I don't want to die." The lady said, "You are fine baby. I promise." As she was helping me out of the car, I had no clue where my glasses were and the lady who was there found them. She helped me to the side of the road and I noticed what the car looked like. I cried. All I could think of was what was going to happen to TJ.

I never got the woman's name or even her husband, but they both stayed with me until the ambulance showed up. Everyone passing by was amazed I walked away from such a terrible accident. One of the firemen said, "You must have a guardian angel looking out for you because there should be no reason why you're still here." I just looked at him, not because of how he said it, but what he said was true. Miller finally made it to the scene and he said the same thing. Miller said, "Sporty, God truly had you covered." I was still trying to wrap my mind around what happened, and the driver of the garbage truck finally came up to me. The driver said, "The only reason why I didn't come over sooner to check on you was because I knew that I killed you." After he made his statement, he walked off. I didn't have a chance to say anything because the conversation happened so quickly. All I remember saying next was, "God I guess this means you're not letting out of my assignment of becoming a minister."

EMS examined me and then the dreaded part happened. I had to be strapped down to the board for transport to the hospital. I was nervous because I didn't have any insurance and was already in the hole since it was six months of being out of work. I finally made it to the emergency room and I had a major panic attack and was given oxygen to breathe. After the oxygen, I passed back out because I was still strapped to the board. Okay, I didn't handle the situation well, but what did you expect since so many things were happening all at once.

I was placed in an examining room and more tests were done to make sure I was okay. As I was lying on the table all I could do was laugh because of the date being September 8, 2010. Since walking in my calling, I had become fascinated with what Biblical numbers meant. The number nine means Divine completeness from the Father, the number eight means the number of new beginnings and ten means the number for testimony. In essence, I was chosen as a willing vessel to show how God still performs miracles and I needed to share with everyone the experience I went through.

Once the tests were completed I was placed in another room and the attendant said, "You sure are lucky." As he was talking one of the elders from church walked in and said, "No, she is blessed by the favor of God's hand." Elder Mavis gave me a big hug and said, "I heard what happened and I got here as soon as I could." It felt good to have someone from the church to show up since my parents still didn't know what was going on. I called my mother on the phone and she said, "I can't talk to you now since I'm trying to find out what is going on with Denise" and hung up the phone, thinking it was someone else. All I could do was start laughing again because this was all God and I had absolutely nothing to do with it.

I was sent back to the first room I was initially in and my pastor showed up. His facial expression changed, and he stated, "Pastor Miller needs to work on his delivery skills because I thought I was coming to see your eye hanging from the socket." Immediately, both Pastor and Elder Mavis prayed over me and it felt good to see them both. I was discharged about two hours later, and Elder Mavis took me home. I was told they couldn't find anything wrong with me and to take it easy for the next few days. I knew why I was discharged because I didn't have any insurance and I knew when I got the bill it probably would send me right back to the hospital.

TJ heard the news and he started to cry so I did my best to calm down. My parents finally made it in from Baton Rouge and all I could do was lay in the bed to digest all that happened throughout the day. I mean getting hit by a garbage truck was not on my to-do list. I was grateful to be in one piece and still there to take care of my son. I only rested for a day because now I had to figure out what my next move would be.

I rested all day Thursday and was back at it on Friday. My mother said, "You are crazy to even want to get back behind the wheel." I looked at her and said, "If not now, when?" I told you I was stubborn and I wasn't going to let what happened stop me from doing what I needed to do. I returned to work and my boss' first question was, "Are you going to hold me liable?" I said, "Why would I? You can relax because I'm not coming after you." This made me mad that he even asked me such a question and I decided to quit because I didn't want to have any foolishness come about from it. So, there I was back to being unemployed and now I needed a game plan on what to do next.

A few weeks had passed and I called a friend who was a lawyer to find out the best way to handle the accident. She told me she couldn't do anything, but she knew of a great lawyer who could. The lawyer's name was Jhase Lowery, and he was known for handling personal injury cases. I met with Mr. Lowery. I explained what happened and he gladly took on the case. Mr. Lowery stated, "Please know that it's going to take time with the case since I have to be able to prove that it was negligence on the driver's part, and not the actual company." I didn't care and all I was looking at was getting a decent amount of money to live off. Being naïve, I listened to people telling me I was going to get a lot of money from the lawsuit and I might not have to work ever again. Hearing this made me feel good and gave me some hope to accept what I had just been through.

I called Aaron and shared with him what happened with the accident and his only response was, "So how much money do you think you will get from the lawsuit?" I was shocked he didn't even ask about how I was doing and immediately went to the money. I told Aaron I had another call coming in and that I would call him right back. I was angry and realized Aaron was just like everybody else and he didn't care about me either.

Weeks passed, and I started to feel really bad. I wasn't sure if it was from not having anything to do or from the accident. It got to the point where I couldn't even dress myself, and I had no choice but to ask TJ to help me. I love getting my nails done and as I was on my way to the bathroom, I hit the return vent and ripped my entire nail off. I yelled for TJ to help me and he said, "Ma, you look drunk. Are you alright?" I wasn't alright and something needed to be done. Once TJ helped me to the bed I called Jhase to find out if he could schedule a doctor's appointment so I could find out what was going on with me. Jhase scheduled the appointment and all I could do was wait. I had a second chance at life, but it sure was a doozy, this ride. I wanted off, and wanted off quickly.

I met with the doctor and was told I needed surgery on my neck and I gladly told the doctor that wasn't an option. I was also told the back quadrant of my brain had some damage because of the late on site concussion and it would affect my short-term memory. It all made sense now, but I wasn't having anyone operating on my neck and I didn't care who got mad. I had come home not knowing what I needed to do and was all over the place trying to figure out my next move.

Remember after the accident I was without a car and my mother was on me about her credit. How would I get around? I had to turn the rental car in and I refused to go to my mother again. I went back to my lawyer friend and we worked out a deal for me to purchase her father's car. Her father had passed, and when the money would come in I would pay her for the car. It seemed fair, but as always, nothing goes right for me.

The day had come for me to be licensed as a minister. I waited until the week before to tell my mother because I knew she was going to have some problem with it. My mother said, "I don't know if we can make it, and it will be late and then we still have to get on the road to come back." I left it alone and I had to do what God had called me to do. And if my parents weren't going to be there I would still be alright. For Christ, I live and for Christ I die, and I have made up my mind. The ceremony had started and while sitting on the pulpit I noticed a few things which caught me off guard. I had to do a double take because Jay was sitting out in the congregation and my parents were there too. So, this would have been interesting to see how my parents would receive what God has called me to be.

I was proud of myself now that I was a minister and didn't care if I didn't make anyone happy. It was something different and maybe my life would start to change. I was licensed in November, and now it is January of 2011. I didn't know which way was up, but I knew I had to keep pushing so I wouldn't lose my mind. I would search and search for a job and nothing would come, and all I could do was lay in the bed because I was depressed. This lasted for weeks and then I received a call about a job.

I started working at a storage company and it was part-time, but it was work. I just needed something to do so I wouldn't lose my mind and to stay busy. Me working at a storage company? Never say what you won't do because God will set it up and show you that you will. It was interesting, and doing manual labor showed me I wasn't as bougie as I thought I was. I stayed at the storage company longer than I wanted, but I experienced a lot which stuck with me.

My supervisor, Gabby, was wonderful and she had become a good friend especially since I was going through so much at the time. And there was also Dale, who was the assistant manager. Dale made my days interesting with his cantankerous attitude and he was as sweet as pie to me, but when it came to Gabby…Well, it was a different story. I ended up working many shifts with Dale and I learned more than I cared to mention, but I would keep all that I learned in my back pocket. Since I only worked part-time I continued to search for another job because, after all, I didn't want to let TJ down ever.

I finally heard from my lawyer friend and she told me I could come and get the car. The PT loser, as TJ called it, and this car gave me the blues. I spent more money than I could imagine to keep the car running. I was still working part time at a storage company and the little money I was making went right into keeping the car running. This went on for months until I was pulled over by the police. It was nothing but the hand of God. I didn't go to jail because the tags were expired and when I called my lawyer friend, she wouldn't answer the phone. I was set up by God to do what I said I wasn't going to do, and it was to go back to my mother for help. I told God I would never go back, but He sent me straight to her.

I called my mother to ask if she could help me now that I didn't have a way to get around. The conversation was so harsh I dare not repeat it, but all I could do was cry once I got off the phone. I then asked God, "Why did I need to go through this, and it's not fair the way she treats me." All I did was cry for hours to the point I made myself sick to the stomach. My parents showed up at the house with my mother's car, the Corolla, and gave me the keys. All I could do was say thank you because I didn't know what just happened, but I thanked God for the blessing. I was at a loss for words, but it continued to get better. Not financially, but by the way my life was going.

I could say now God would lead us to certain places in order to get healed from our past pain. While at the storage company I had run into Robert. Remember, Robert was from high school and a part of the rumors that had everyone wanted to stay away from me. I tried to ignore him and hoped he wouldn't see me, but it didn't work. Robert asked if we could go outside to talk. I told Gabby I would be right back. Robert said, "I want to apologize for how Jeremy treated you, and he was the one spreading the rumors about you in high school." All I could do was just stand there and stare because he didn't have to tell me, especially after all this time. Robert also said, "I tried to stop him, but he threatened me too. I'm truly sorry and I hope this will fix things. By the way, Jeremy's a pastor now." With all this coming at me at once I couldn't do anything but tell him, "Thank You" and go into one of the storage hallways and cry. It made me feel better, but I did wish it was Jeremy and not Robert telling me all this.

Things were going well at the storage company and then I had an opportunity to go back into social work. I was excited I could go back into what I loved and didn't care how I got back in. The new job was doing permanent supportive housing, and I started immediately. Now the concern was whether I could do both jobs since I was at the storage company part-time. I could probably swing it, and if I couldn't then I would leave the storage company.

I was able to swing both jobs for a while and I did it for nearly a year. I did it until it was time for TJ to graduate from high school. Aaron was still in the picture and we discussed me moving to Atlanta. I had everyone aware I was trying to move to Atlanta and everyone at church told me that I wasn't going, and I didn't believe them. Miller told me, "We prayed about it and you're not going anywhere." I didn't believe him and continued with my plans of moving. Everything went well until Aaron told me not to move out to Atlanta out of the blue. I was convinced then it was God and never questioned what Aaron said to me. My feelings for Aaron had changed and the move to Atlanta was no longer a concern. I left the storage company, but Gabby still thought I was still moving to Atlanta because I didn't know how to tell her everything had fallen apart.

17

MAKING A MOVE

TJ was about to graduate from high school and he was accepted to an extremely popular university in Baton Rouge. I was excited, and he was excited too, until he received some devastating news. TJ found out his dorm room assignment was messed up and he wouldn't be able to stay on campus. The thought of him living with my parents definitely wasn't going to work out. TJ made it known he didn't want to live with his grandparents. I wanted him to enjoy college, so I decided to move to Baton Rouge. It might be for the best especially with Atlanta not being an option anymore. I immediately started searching for apartments and had only a few months to do it.

I drove my mother crazy because I would drag her with me. I knew we didn't have the best relationship, but she knew her way around Baton Rouge. Her insight would make the process easy, so we searched until I found the ideal spot. It was pricey, but the apartment was off Interstate 10 and it made getting to work in New Orleans a straight shot.

Everything was falling into place and I only wanted the best for my son. I knew if he lived with my parents he would either go crazy or start using drugs...lol. He was still trying to find himself, and my parents definitely would have made it hard for him to do. The move was a go and moving to Baton Rouge would take place a week after my birthday. What a wonderful way to start my 39th birthday and to do so in a new city.

It was a moving day and I was still wrapping my mind around moving to Baton Rouge. I got over Atlanta, but part of me was still mad about why Aaron didn't want me to come. Moving took the entire day, and with the rain, made me question if I was doing the right thing. TJ and his friends did most of the work which put me at ease, but unpacking was never the fun part. Unpacking took all night and I was ready for it to be over. I didn't bother TJ anymore and took it upon myself to put up everything where it belonged. Baton Rouge was an adjustment for the both of us, but TJ proved to me he would do just fine his first semester of college.

As TJ got adjusted to college, I got adjusted to the daily commute. This move was harder than I thought, and I only signed my lease for six months because I didn't think living in Baton Rouge would work right away. I needed to have a backup plan if things fell apart so I could be ready to move back to New Orleans.

TJ managed to survive his first semester of school and I managed to survive living in Baton Rouge. I changed my mind and realized living in Baton Rouge wasn't so bad, and I needed to give it a chance. TJ found out at the end of his first semester he had the opportunity to stay in the upper class men's dorm since the school realized the error was on their part. I was excited for him and this would give him the opportunity to experience something totally different which would allow him to hang out with the seniors. This was good news; for the first time I would be on my own. I was not sure if I was ready for it. I went from growing up in my parents' house, to being married, back to their house, and then living on my own. It was a different ride, but I was never alone since TJ always rode shotgun and that would be his permanent spot.

Remember the lawsuit? Well, it finally came in, and I was disappointed. It was now two years later and I figured with it taking so long I would walk away with a decent amount of money to live off of. What a disappointing thought. After paying my mother for the Corolla, getting a car, and the lawyer getting his cut, there wasn't anything left over. Whoever said that you get paid from lawsuits quickly lied, but some money was better than nothing! TJ was happy he had a car and we didn't have to depend on my mother for anything. Things were looking up and I was preparing for the next transition of finally living on my own, but only time would tell.

18

SPREADING MY WINGS

TJ finally moved into the upper class men's dorm and I was all by myself. For the first month, it was uncomfortable, and it was almost as if I was waiting for TJ to show up each night. I finally settled in though, and started enjoying being by myself. Before I knew it those four months had flown by.

The spring semester was over, and TJ was back home. It was short-lived, but I was glad to have him home. During the summer things had become interesting, and TJ presented me with some news. I didn't know what the news could be, and I must be honest the first thing popped in my head was he must have done something wrong. What he asked turned out to be something completely different. TJ asked if his friend, Devin, could stay for the summer. I was extremely happy about having him, and knew he wouldn't be a problem. TJ and Devin had been friends since high school and I always considered him to be my son. The running joke was that he got his color from his dad's side of the family.

Spending the summer with my boys made me feel good, and it didn't matter that I was single. I was a happy mom. TJ stated, "Mother, I think I will stay home and not go back to the dorms since it's too much trouble." I agreed and told TJ, "You can stay as long as you want, especially if it will help out with school." So, the decision was made, and TJ stayed home while trying to figure out what to do for his sophomore year.

Throughout high school, TJ was in the Air Force Reserve Officer Training Corps (ROTC) program, and decided he wanted to make it a career. Since being in college he held true to it and the ROTC would occupy most of his time. It was cool, and I was able to hang out with Devin more. We never know what God has for us to do so being obedient is always key. This was part of my assignment and I didn't even know it. One evening Devin and I talked for hours, and listening made a difference in his life that night. It was a necessity that Devin was there, and opening my house to him only made my obedience the opportunity for him to talk about a painful part of his life.

I learned a lot from the boys that summer and I think that they learned a little something from me too. I realized I had started to spread my wings and was walking in who God had called me to be. It was still confusing, but I was learning that God wasn't the author of confusion, and that I had to tune into Him more. I just didn't know how much more I was going to experience in the months to come.

The summer had ended, and TJ was preparing for his sophomore year. It was a difficult year, but not the way he would have imagined. TJ decided to change his major from Mechanical Engineering to Political Science. When TJ presented his logic to me, it all made sense. TJ said, "How can I argue against something I don't know anything about, but if I major in the subject then I would have a good rebuttal about why I don't like what goes on."

It made sense, so I told him, "Baby I will always support everything you want to do."

TJ loved being a part of the Air Force ROTC, but unfortunately it didn't love him in return. TJ had come home upset, saying his Commanding Officer was giving him the blues and everything he did was not right. All I could do was tell him to talk to someone else and see if they could help him talk to his CO, and that maybe things would get better for him. TJ spoke with some of his peers and things calmed down for a while. I prayed things would get better for him since this was all he ever wanted to do.

Being on my own wasn't easy, but I was doing my best to be there for my son. Ted wasn't around much so I could never show TJ how to be a man. His being in the ROTC was the only way I knew TJ would get the push he needed to go in the right direction. After all, I wanted him to succeed since I was told I could never be allowed to be a part of the military. I guess I was doing what my mother said, and was living vicariously through him since I wasn't allowed to go into the Air Force in college. I continued to support TJ in everything he did and since I couldn't give him much financially, this was the next best thing.

Still single and nothing changed, one of my friends from church decided she wanted to "hook me up" with one of her husband's friends. My friend, Rochelle, and I sang in the choir together and I agreed since my love life was no such thing. Honestly, I wasn't impressed, but still agreed to go out on a date with him. Rochelle suggested we go on a double date after church, so it wouldn't feel awkward and if I didn't like him, I wouldn't be stuck with him by myself.

It was Sunday after church and I went to Rochelle's house. Once there Rochelle said, "John has to bring Bishop home, so I decided to cook instead. Are you okay with that?" Of course, I really didn't want to go on the date in the first place and was only doing it to be nice.

Rochelle said, "As soon as John drops Bishop off, he is going to pick up Al and then we will have dinner." We talked until John made it to the house, and when I saw Al, I was not impressed and knew this was going to be a waste of my time.

We ate dinner and I kept the small talk to a minimum. The only thing that saved me was it was football season and a game was on. John noticed I wasn't happy and suggested he would go to the store. John said, "Imma get some more water and drinks. Al why don't you come with me?" I was glad and told Rochelle, "I'm mad at you and John for even thinking I would be attracted to someone like that." In the middle of our conversation the strangest thing happened. Remember the police officer I told you about whose name I didn't know? Well, he walked through the door. He said, "What are you doing here?" I said, "Rochelle is my friend, why wouldn't I be here?" He said, "Well, she's my sister and that's why I'm here?" So, my day turned out better than I imagined.

Rochelle said," How do you know June?" He stated, "I remember now you used to work at the courthouse." He then said, "My name is Vince, but they call me June, short for Junior." I smiled to myself since he didn't come alone. We talked. The woman he was with appeared to be disgusted. We continued to talk until Vince got a phone call and went outside to answer it. Once he went outside the woman stated, "So I guess you already had sex with him?" Rochelle said, "Please stop Kimmy. Be nice." Kimmy stated, "That's all he does, and if he hasn't slept with her yet, he will because he's showing too much interest in her."

I knew it was time for me to leave and I definitely wanted to leave before John got back with Al. I told Rochelle I would call her later and thanked her for dinner. I casually told Kimmy bye and walked out of the door. Vince waved and I got into my car and drove back to Baton Rouge. I smiled all the way home because who would have ever imagined I would run into the New Orleans police officer who was checking me out while I was working at the courthouse.

A few days later there was an event at church and John said, "Can I talk to you?" John stated, "Vince wanted to know if he could have your number, and before I gave it to him I wanted to ask you first." I was excited on the inside, and since we were in church I didn't want to seem desperate. I told John. "Sure, you could give him my number, that's not a problem." This made my night and I waited for Vince to call. Later that night I received a text from Vince to give him a call. We talked on the phone for at least four hours while he was at work. It was an amazing conversation and the start of something new.

Vince and I would spend limited time together, but with him being an officer I was okay with the time spent. My day would be on Sundays since I was in the city for church. He had set up a routine, and I was okay with it not knowing I was one of many on his team. Vince made me feel like I was the only woman in his life and I enjoyed every minute of it when we were together.

A few months had passed, and I was getting ready for my trip in June of 2013 to the Bahamas. One of the women from work, Bobbie, joked about going to the Bahamas and before you knew it the trip was planned. Bobbie said, "Let's get our passports! It's my dream to travel as much as possible." I told Bobbie, "Well, I don't mind the Bahamas, but all that traveling is not for me." The trip was only for a few days, but I had never been out of the country before, so I didn't want to be gone too long for my first time.

It was finally time for the vacation and Vince took us to the airport. I decided to leave my car at his house with the thought that we were getting close. I was now ready to jet set out of the country hoping I would have more fun than I could imagine. We made it to the airport and got out of Vince's truck when he said, "Have fun and I will miss you." Bobbie said, "That is so sweet, and I know that she will miss you too." We both laughed and I gave Vince a kiss.

The Bahamas was such a wonderful experience, from the food to the night life. After we got settled into the hotel it didn't take any time for us to meet some natives when I met Greg, and Bobbie met Marc. Bahamian men were truly different from American men and all I could think about was Vince. When we got to our room it was horrible. We had to switch rooms three separate times because of the mold. I fussed to the point that we got our money back for the room. I initially got sick, but once we were put in a decent room we started to enjoy our trip. Bobbie and I were able to experience the Bahamas from the native perspective, and it spoke volumes giving us the time of our lives. It was better than Vegas and yes,

"What happened in the Bahamas, stayed in the Bahamas."

Our trip was over, and it was time to come back home. I was happy to be back home, not realizing I was going to get the most devastating news ever. I found out my mother had breast cancer and it was stage one. What a wonderful way to end my vacation! After digesting the news, I asked my father, "Why wasn't I told about this sooner?" My father said, "We wanted you to enjoy your trip." What could I say? Turning 40 was not the way I planned it to be. Happy Birthday to me!!!

2013 was an interesting year because my grandmother was also terminally ill. Being the oldest had taken its toll. My grandmother was 99 and suffered from Alzheimer's disease. Let me paint the picture. My mother had breast cancer, my grandmother had Alzheimer's disease, and my father was falling apart. Both his wife and his mother were affected and I had to keep him together. My job was never done and from all the stress I had developed chronic migraines. I shouldn't have tried to spread my wings so quickly and should have just kept them together because I obviously was not flying in the right direction.

My headaches were so bad that I started missing days from work and my boss wasn't happy at all. I told my boss I was dealing with my mother and grandmother, so she wouldn't think I was just trying to skip work. My mother had her mastectomy in July, and my grandmother died in August, a week after my birthday. See, I told you 2013 was a rough year. I was on overload and God was the only one I could go to. I eventually left the job in October of 2013 because of all the stress. I was so overwhelmed I needed a break to get my head together.

19

UNDERSTANDING THE JOURNEY

Things started to settle down again, but not for long. TJ adjusted to the change in his major and I was good with living in Baton Rouge. Thanksgiving was over, and we were preparing for Christmas. It was Sunday, December 1, 2013 and my life made another unexpected change. The day before, the actor Paul Walker and his driver were killed in a car accident.

The actor's car slammed into a tree and both he and the driver were killed upon impact. That morning as I was leaving out for church TJ jokingly said, "Don't go out and hit any trees." I smiled and said, "Don't worry I will be careful on the way to church."

It was Communion Sunday and being a minister, I had to wear clergy attire which consisted of a black suit and black shirt, with either a tab or a roman collar. I was in full dress and headed out the door like I normally would each Sunday. As I mentioned before, it took an hour to get to New Orleans, but my life took another turn and things changed. I was driving on the highway taking my regular route and I blacked out or at least I was told I did by the state trooper. The state trooper mentioned I'd spun out of control hitting a tree. He then stated, "I don't know how you did it but I'm glad you did, or we would be pulling your body out of the swamp."

I had no clue what the state trooper was talking about. The state trooper then asked, "Are you okay? I called EMS and they are on their way." I remember asking "What happened?" The state trooper stated, "All I remember was you were trying to avoid the car that pulled over in front of you and your car spun out of control, hit my cruiser, and then you hit the tree." I asked the state trooper to call my father to let him know what happened. EMS showed up to the scene and I started feeling extremely weak.

EMS asked, "Were you drinking?" I looked at him with a crazy stare and he said, "Sorry ma'am, but I have to ask the question due to the nature of the accident." EMS then stated, "Do you realize that there are alligators in there and we could be fishing you out right now." Again, I just looked at him wondering why he was even employed because his bedside manner sucked.

EMS was able to get me out of the car and strapped me to a board. I was en-route to the hospital, not remembering anything and woke up seeing my father at the side of the bed. My father said, "You are in the emergency room and they ran a test. The only thing they could find was you lost oxygen to the brain causing you to blackout." I figured it came from the previous accident and left it alone. My father drove me to their house and he said, "We'll worry about the car tomorrow. You need some rest." Once I made it to the house, I called Vince to let him know what happened and he seemed unconcerned to what happened to me.

Still trying to wrap my mind around what took place, two weeks later I received a letter saying I was a candidate for ordination to become an elder in my church. I started asking God what was going on since none of this was making sense to me anymore. All I wanted to do was go back to being normal and maybe some of these things would stop happening to me. My mother didn't speak to me much, and I did my best to explain to TJ why all of this was going on. It was hard to explain to him when I didn't have a clue myself.

I stayed focused and started to prepare for my ordination. I hoped once I became an elder I would get some clarification to why I was going through all of this. My pastor told me I would lose a lot of people along the way and it was definitely happening. I was spending less time with Vince, and I knew it had to do with the journey God had chosen for me. My mother was only speaking to me when necessary and I started working at a car dealership. I hated the direction my life was going in, but I knew I couldn't give up because of TJ.

After leaving the job I was stressed at, my old boss filed a complaint against me and I couldn't practice social work until the investigation was over. It hit me like a ton of bricks. Three months later I started working at the dealership. After the news I stayed at the dealership for two months, but it felt like a lifetime. I worked long hours and I wasn't making any money and found myself asking my parents for money again. My mother's tone was so harsh, but what could I do; I couldn't financially take care of myself or be there for TJ for that matter.

I cried out to God for help because I couldn't do this any longer and I felt I was in the wilderness by myself. It was January of 2014 and it never snowed in Baton Rouge, but to our surprise the city was covered in snow. I knew I couldn't take being at the dealership when we were told we had to work during the snowstorm. I wasn't driving in the snow and prayed the investigation would be over soon. I knew I would be fired but would take the chance and not go out in the bad weather. I survived too much, and how would it look for the snow to be the reason for my demise?!

I still had a job and a few weeks later I got a call from my sister regarding a job. Kristen told me I needed to call this girl as soon as I got off the phone with her. Earlier in the month my prayers were answered, as it was determined I didn't do anything wrong as it related to my past job. The complaints made by a previous supervisor were determined to be false, allowing me to practice social work again. The investigator said, "It's off the record; you must have pissed your boss off for her to file this report because there isn't anything I could find that you did wrong." During the interview I said to the investigator, "She is 26 and I'm 40, and I've been practicing just as long as she has been living on this earth and she got mad when I questioned her about a particular client." The investigator said, "You are cleared and are able to practice again."

I immediately made the call after getting off the phone with my sister. I spoke with Angela and was told what I needed to do as it related to the position. I didn't care where it was as long as I could get away from the car dealership. It was case management and in the field of social work and I quit the dealership as soon as I got the okay to start. I spoke to Angela on a Monday and quit the Friday of the same week. I was so happy to be gone and didn't mind commuting to New Orleans again.

I enjoyed being at the new job and I was doing mental health rehabilitation. I was only at the new job for a few weeks and I knew it was better than working at the dealership. I enjoyed having the freedom of coming and going until my car decided to do its own thing. I was driving on the interstate and my car shut down on the bridge. I did my best to get the car over to the emergency lane without being hit by an eighteen-wheeler. I called Vince to come and get me and he said, "Call your sister to come and get you." I was pissed because I didn't believe he said that to me. Once I got the car to the nearest dealership in New Orleans, I called the dealership in Baton Rouge to fuss about what took place with the car. By the time I finished arguing the dealership had no choice but to pay for the repairs. I believed in my mind the car shutting down was a result of the dealership not repairing the car correctly after the incident with hitting the tree. The dealership did a horrible job and refused to admit to it, but I held them accountable.

A few months later Miller had a preaching engagement and asked me to come see him. Miller mentioned he wanted some of the church family to be there, so he would feel comfortable, so I agreed to go. My running joke was that unless God would come down and tap me on my shoulder I wouldn't walk in my gift as a prophet. The date was August 8, 2014 and after the service the head pastor started to prophesy to everyone, and this was the night which confirmed who I was. Pastor Jones finally got to me and she blew my mind. She said, "God is proud of you, but you need to walk in the gift He has given you." I was surprised because this woman didn't even know who I was, and she was telling me things which happened in my life. Pastor Jones continued to say, "God is telling me to pass my mantle to you, and from this day forward you have to walk in who God has called you to be." I was amazed by what was said. I immediately started to cry because I knew God was holding me accountable for my gift. There was just one thing; my pastor said no one was released to do anything without being told by him first. Until he gave the okay, then I couldn't walk in my gift, while being under his covering.

The following month we had our monthly ministry meeting at church and during the meeting my pastor came out of his office and said, "I'm giving my blessing to walk in who God has called you to be, and whoever this is for-God is pleased." I knew my pastor was speaking to me and I had no choice but to be who God had called me to be. So many things continued to happen and now I was charged with walking in my gift of prophecy.

I was still dealing with what was said and the following week Miller decided to take me to lunch to talk about how I was feeling. While there, we talked about what happened with Vince. Miller told me something which stuck with me for a very long time. Miller said, "A man will make time for what he wants, and if he doesn't then you should have your answer." I didn't want to hear it, but I knew he was telling the truth. I made it up my mind I wasn't going to go anywhere I wasn't invited or be with anyone who didn't want to be with me. I kept my distance from Vince and decided to leave him alone.

After getting my car fixed it was time to get my oil changed so I decided to take my car to the same dealership I left. I saw the guy I used to work with, Chris, and told him what happened with the car. Chris suggested that I needed to trade the car in and see if I could get something else. I agreed and was surprised when I was able to leave the dealership with a new car. It was September of 2014 and I left the dealership with a 2014 Chevy Cruze. I was actually glad I didn't have the Camaro anymore. This was definitely one lemon that I couldn't make lemonade with.

The following week I was to teach Bible Study and I testified how I was able to leave the dealership with a new car knowing my credit was horrible. I explained to everyone that God will do some things which will mess your head up, especially when we have no choice but to let others know it was Him in the first place. In two weeks, it would be time to take my ordination exam and after leaving Bible study, I would be up studying until it was time to take the exam.

The exam was now over, and I was extremely tired. I was asked to stay in the city and I told everyone I was going home to sleep in my own bed, and that I would let everyone know when I made it to Baton Rouge. It was the longest drive ever and I hit an alligator on the way home. After the accident I thought I hit someone and was scared because I didn't know what to do and figured I would be going to jail. I couldn't believe the car was destroyed after only two weeks and I didn't know what to do. OnStar called the police and while I was waiting, all I could think about was that if I was in the Camaro I would probably be dead because the car would have flipped over.

The State Trooper showed up and asked, "Do you know what you hit?" I told him emotionally, "I hope it wasn't a person." The State Trooper laughed and said, "Come take a walk with me." I got out of the car and walked over to see a 7-foot alligator on the side of the road. The state trooper said, "You're lucky. Since it's mating season, all he was trying to do was get to the swamp on the other side." I said, "Well, he won't be mating tonight or ever again." The state trooper told me, "Since it's at night I won't give you a ticket, but if it was during the day, you could have gone to jail since the gator is considered endangered."

I called my father and the state trooper stayed with me until he got there. It took my father a while to find me since I wasn't in the best place on the side of the highway. We were parked off mile-marker 198, and the only light was the state trooper's cruiser. My father finally made it and I found out he knew the state trooper. The two of them talked for 30 minutes and I decided to get in his car because I didn't want any other alligators coming to get me since I had killed one of their own. It was 2:00 am after the accident was finally cleared and I only wanted to get in my bed. As always, my mother didn't speak to me for about three months and honestly, I didn't even know why. I started to question again what I have done wrong to cause all this drama and it didn't seem to stop.

Things were getting stranger to the point I didn't know how to deal with what was going on around me. Michael Brown was murdered in August of 2014 and the world seemed to be upside down. I was sitting in the pulpit in October of 2014 to preach and it was as if I could hear the rioting in Ferguson, MO. I asked the other elder sitting next to me if she heard anything and she said, "I don't hear anything." I turned to Keisha again saying, "Are you sure, because it sounds like it's coming out of the speakers?" Keisha looked at me and said, "I don't hear anything, and I promise that the only thing coming out of the speakers is music." I got up to preach, still hearing all the noise. It bothered me, but I didn't allow my emotions to show what I was thinking. By the time I made it home I laid prostrate on the floor before God because the rioting only got louder in my ears and it started to scare me. While down there 1 Corinthians 14: 3-4 had come to mind. It states, [3] "But the one who prophesies speaks to people for their strengthening, encouragement and comfort. [4] Anyone who speaks in a tongue edifies themselves, but the one who prophesies edifies the church." Then 2 Chronicles 7: 14 followed next. It states, [14] "if my people, who are called by my name, will humble themselves and pray and seek my face and turn from their wicked ways, then I will hear from heaven, and I will forgive their sin and will heal their land."

I figured out what was going on and had tapped into what the people were feeling, and I could actually hear and feel their pain. Before I got up the Holy Spirit told me one last thing and it was to leave Vince alone. It hurt my heart, but I had to be obedient to what was told to me. So, the next day I sent Vince a 14-paragraph email to explain why I needed to leave him alone. It was especially hard since his birthday was coming up in a few weeks.

I did my best to avoid Vince, but when his birthday had come I was caught up with everything he put on social media. I couldn't help myself and I knew I was being disobedient. I limited my contact, but he made it his business to keep in touch which made me weak. I knew what I had to do and God was holding me accountable for keeping my distance. And I did okay until I was invited to a gala and I was persuaded to invite him.

It was January of 2015 and Vince went to the gala with me. I truly enjoyed myself and realized we had never gone anywhere together, and this was the first time. At the end of the night Vince stated, "Princess I have to go to work and I'll call you later." I knew I wouldn't see or hear from him, but at least I got to spend part of the night with him. I felt like a true princess and he had to leave before the clock struck midnight.

I continued to avoid Vince after the gala, and did okay until Father's Day. On Father's Day Vince called and asked me to bring him something to eat. He was on a detail located on the Riverview and when I got to where he was I told Vince, "My eyeballs are sweating." Vince then said, "Dee don't say that out loud because that sounds crazy." I told him, "I didn't care and that's what was going on." We talked for a while and once I left I didn't hear from him until a week later. Vince had come to the apartment, but only because he needed to pick his son up from Alexandria. I remember it was June 25, 2015 and I left Vince at the apartment since I needed to go to work. Later that day, I called him to make sure he was on the road to pick up his son. When he answered he said the strangest thing, "I turned the air down because I was cold." That was weird because he was never cold. I made it to the apartment. It was extremely hot, and it felt as if a strange spirit was in the apartment. I called Vince, but he didn't answer so I went to the store to get more batteries for the thermostat. After I changed the batteries I immediately started praying to change the atmosphere in the apartment. From that moment on my life was completely different and I prepared myself for more to come.

I started a new job and had only been there a few months when I got the news. It was a Sunday and I was on my way to church when Miller called me on the phone. Miller said, "Did you hear about Vince?" I immediately asked him, "What happened?" Miller stated, "I hate to be the one to tell you, but Vince was hit on the bridge." I couldn't catch my breath and was trying to focus so I could get to church. Once I made it there I kneeled at the altar and the Holy Spirit brought back to me he wasn't mine in the first place and how I had to let him go.

After church, I went to the hospital to see Vince and everything I ever thought about had come true. There were so many women at the hospital, which brought light to why I needed to leave him alone. Interestingly enough, I met and had become friends with one of the women Vince was dealing with. Her name was Nichelle and we found ourselves going to the funeral together. It took a while for me to digest Vince was gone and I would never see him again. Two weeks earlier Vince was dealing with the death of another officer and I sent him a text informing him about allowing God to be in control and no matter the outcome God had him. I never realized I was preparing for the new journey in his life.

It had been a few weeks since Vince's death, and I decided I would take a break from dating to find out who I was. My track record with men had always been bad and losing Vince showed it to be true. I was starting to think maybe I'm supposed to be by myself and I was starting to accept the fact myself. It was August again and it was my birthday. It was suggested by a friend to consider online dating because I didn't need to be by myself.

I blew it off and I ignored it for a while when my friend suggested online dating again. I remembered it well because it was my baby sister's birthday. I decided to try it, and like everything else it turned out to be a disaster. I dealt with four different guys separately online, and trust me all four had foolishness with them. The first one was paranoid. The second one didn't know who he wanted to be and went by two different names. The third one was a deacon and told me I spent too much time at church. And the fourth one, well, we decided there wasn't a connection between us. So much for online dating! It was truly a waste of my time, so being single didn't seem so bad.

I had survived the craziness or at least I thought. I made one more attempt at online dating and it was the worst move I had ever made. I met a guy online in February of 2016 and he made me think life was going to be wonderful and after a month he disappeared. I thought something was truly wrong with me and it was only a trick of the enemy. I moved on and made it up in my mind to enjoy my life instead. It was Resurrection Sunday and I received a disturbing text around 2:00 am and thought it was a dream since it was early in the morning. The texts continued to come in and they stated,

"If you don't send me $10,000.00, I will hurt you and your son." I was scared and I immediately started praying. I went to church and pulled the executive pastor on the side and told her what was going on. We prayed for nothing to harm me and TJ, and left the situation with God, knowing He would handle it.

I got home and told TJ the entire story. He was mad, but my son transformed into the person God had called him to be and he handled the situation. TJ did the research and found out I was scammed or "catfished" and it started in Nigeria with the hopes of scamming money. I went as far as calling the Sheriff's department and they did absolutely nothing. TJ did more to defuse the situation and the Sheriff's department made it seem as if this matter was a waste of their time. I followed everything TJ told me to ensure I wouldn't be caught up in this type of situation again.

Once it was over TJ apologized for fussing at me, but I apologized because I was out of line for my actions, and he only did what was required of him. I knew my son was walking in who God called him to be and the military was a part of him. TJ went through a lot with the Air Force, but the Army was truly in his future.

2016 was not turning out to be the best year for me and I was ready for the year to be over. It was only April, but it felt like the year was lasting forever. It was the most devastating time for TJ, but he held up better than I thought. April 8, 2016 would be a day TJ would never forget. It was a Friday and I was surprised that all my appointments were canceled. I looked at it as a day to take a break and I didn't have to get on the highway. I tried to rest, but resting was the last thing I did.

I received a phone call indicating Ted had died from a massive heartache and my only concern was getting to TJ. I needed to be in the city and not in New Orleans because TJ needed me more than ever. TJ's stepmother, Connie, informed me of the news and once I got off the phone with her I immediately called TJ's uncle, Eddie to find out more. I told Eddie I needed to be the one to call TJ and give him the news, and not anyone else. I immediately called TJ to let him know about his father. I'm known for being straight-forward and I was direct when telling TJ about Ted. He immediately passed out and whoever took the phone told me I needed to get to the school ASAP. While en-route, TJ called and said, "Mother I'm alright, and you don't have to come. I'm good." I said, "I need to put my eyes on you to make sure. I will be there in a few."

Once I got to the school TJ seemed to be okay, but I wasn't sure. We talked for a while and then he said, "Mother I'm good, but if something were to happen to you; y'all would have to put me on an island, because I would be no more good." We laughed and then he said, "Mother, you can leave because I need to get back to my meeting." I agreed and I walked back to the car. I said, "Call me when you need me, and I don't care what I'm doing I will stop and talk to you."

What a day. I knew I needed to be there for TJ more than ever because he was strong like me, but it was still his father. Ted was from Jackson, MS so we had to prepare to go to the funeral and I knew that day would be hard. TJ felt overwhelmed, not by the death of his father, but by the family pulling on him to contribute to the funeral costs. TJ was so angry, and he had a right to be since Ted never did much for him. As April 20 th approached TJ didn't show any emotions and I knew better because grief comes in various stages, but I wanted him to show at least something.

The day of the funeral, I asked Eddie to keep his eyes on TJ and to allow him to do what he wanted since I didn't want to push him. I went to Jackson with my father, and TJ drove on his own. Again, I didn't push it because I didn't want him to have a meltdown. The good thing was that he wasn't graduating as graduation was pushed to the next year. It was stressful, but not having to deal with graduation was one less thing to worry about. As I said earlier it was only April and I was truly ready for the year to be over with. Maybe 2017 would be a better year, and it was my constant prayer.

20

PREPARING FOR THE TRANSITION

I survived the incident of online dating and made myself a promise I would leave the online dating alone. I focused on my job more and being off the road made things better for me. I was preparing for another journey which led to another ride on the roller coaster. It was August of 2016 and it rained so much in Baton Rouge everyone wanted it to stop.

It was the day before my birthday and it had rained nonstop the entire week. I completed an intake with a client and decided not to go out of the city, because I didn't want to get caught in an area that flooded. I called my mother to let her know I wasn't going to Lutcher because of the weather and I was going home. As I was getting off the bridge and sitting at the light, I was rear-ended. I called my mother back to tell her what happened. I told her to tell my father, so he could come to the accident. The area was known for weekly accidents, but it was hard to avoid since it was the exit to my apartment. My father got to the scene of the accident and he asked me to get out of the car, but I couldn't because my legs were numb. The state trooper handled the accident, and I wondered again why I was constantly going through all of this.

As always, I was stubborn and didn't want to go to the hospital. I didn't have insurance, and I did all I could to avoid the trip to the hospital. After we were free to leave the scene my father said, "You are going to urgent care, so we can make sure that you're okay." What could I do but say, "Okay" We were then on our way to urgent care. I was examined, and the doctor told me I would be sore, and to take the medication as prescribed. What a wonderful way to start my 43rd birthday, with the rain, and in bed.

It was my birthday, but my body was telling me something totally different. I got the medication, got some donuts, and yes, I went back to bed. Later during the day, I got a call from my cousin Chris, telling me I needed to leave the apartment because the water was coming up fast and I didn't need to get trapped back there. I lived on the first floor, so I definitely didn't need to be trapped after the accident the day before.

As I was leaving the interstate was down to one lane and my normal ten-minute commute to my parents took me 45 minutes. All I could think was, "I hope this isn't another Katrina." As I was driving I called my co-worker Tracey and she was saying the water was coming up in her neighborhood so fast she and her family were trying to get out. Tracey said, "I have to go because we are trying to get out now while we have a chance." I got to my parents and there were people everywhere, so I went into the bedroom and started watching everything on the news. I fell asleep for a few hours and when I woke up, it was crazy to hear that the city was flooded.

I knew I wasn't going home and my prayer was I still had a home to go to in the morning. TJ was on the other side of town and I knew he would handle the matter well. After all, he was in the Army and slept in the woods for an entire summer. It was now Monday, and getting around the city was ridiculous. I was happy my parents weren't affected, and that TJ was okay too. I had asked TJ to go to the apartment to make sure everything was fine and that, hopefully, I didn't have to start over. I was already dealing with my back and the accident; I didn't need anything else on my plate. Later TJ called to inform me my apartment was dry and that I didn't have any water damage. I was glad to know I didn't have to start over, but my body continued to tell me otherwise.

The city was back on track only after a week, but just as quickly as the water had come in it cleared out. I was in so much pain I called a lawyer to handle the accident. I found out I had a 6-mm herniated disk in my lower back and the lawyer wanted to ensure I received proper compensation for my injuries. I talked to my boss about the accident and he agreed I needed to slow down and that he was trying his best to get me out of the field.

It was TJ's senior year and I was excited my son was preparing to graduate from college. Initially, he was supposed to graduate in 2016 but stayed an extra year to have an officer slot in the Army. TJ had been living on his own for two years and now I had to prepare myself for his leaving to be with Uncle Sam after graduation. This transition would be hard, but I knew he would do well wherever he would be stationed. My baby wasn't a baby anymore and had turned into a grown man. I was so happy knowing he would be serving our country.

TJ did well in his second senior year, but I can't say the same for his mother. My car started making this crazy noise and I took it to the dealership to have it looked at. I was told by the dealership the car was fine, and I had nothing to worry about but if the noise continued to bring the car back. I never got a chance to bring the car back to the dealership when I slammed into a client's house. I left Baton Rouge on a Thursday morning to see a client in a small town. When I pulled into the client's driveway things spiraled out of control. The client lived in a mobile home with her boyfriend's grandmother. I was turning into the client's yard when my car sped up and the breaks didn't work. Before I knew it, I slammed into the mobile home. I was in shock and disbelief as I waited for everyone to come out of the trailer.

When no one had come out, I started to panic thinking they were hurt inside.

I was met by a neighbor and he said, "Ma'am, I saw you trying to stop the car and it wouldn't. I saw you hitting the breaks and it was like the car just kept moving." Another neighbor had shown up and said the same thing. The enemy was messing with my mind and had me thinking I was the one who screwed up. My client finally showed up and told me no one was in the trailer. I started to feel better, but I was still confused and couldn't believe what I was seeing. I got angry and asked God what was going on with me. This seemed like the longest day of my life and I was trying to figure out why I was constantly being targeted. I spoke with the woman who owned the trailer and she said, "Baby as long as you are okay, that's what insurance is for. Nobody was in the trailer and that's all that matters." It was great to hear, but I was still worried about what was going to happen next.

Once things were cleared up I had a rental car and I was back at work the next day. It was going to be a long Thanksgiving, but I had to get things in order. As always, my mother wasn't speaking to me, and I really didn't care because I was trying to think of how I was going to tell the lawyer about the new incident. Only three months had passed since the last accident and now this. The only question I could ask, "What is going to happen next?" I was back to sharing a car with TJ and did all I could do to avoid asking my mother for anything. I made it through the holidays and I was at peace knowing God was in control, and that if He had allowed it was for a reason.

My prayers were answered and I was now in the school system. I was actually happy not to be in the field and that my driving all over the city had been reduced. Me, happy about not driving, turning 43 had shown me I couldn't run like I used to, and the lawyer had stopped me from going to the chiropractor, so not driving was a plus.

I had another problem; I needed to find another place to stay. Things were terrible at the apartment complex and moving was the only option. It was a Thursday night and I started searching for apartments with one particular complex standing out. I got up the next morning, went to a client's house and then to the apartment complex. Once there I got excited because I had actually looked at the complex one before and liked it. The only reason why I didn't move there was because I didn't know Baton Rouge well and needed to be somewhere near to I-10. I made it to the complex at 10:00 am and by 4:30 pm I was told I had the apartment. I knew then it was God, and the Holy Spirit also revealed I would have a car by the end of January. To be more specific by the 28th, and all I could do is trust God.

I was in anticipation of what God was going to do and I was able to see with my own eyes how I should never limit His ability. It was a Thursday again, the 26th of January, and I found out that the day before my GAP insurance had paid off my car. I called my friend, Paul, about getting a car. I spoke with Paul in the morning and by the evening I was going to pick up my new car. Now, let me go back some, when I talked to Paul we were talking about me getting a used car, but I was able to get a brand new one instead. Not only did God show up, but He showed out. The Holy Spirit said by the 28th, and it was the 26th.

Now the other miracle was to wait and see what God was going to do about the apartment since I didn't have the money needed to make the move. The intended move in date was the 7th of March and I knew God had to work it out because again, I was not going to my mother knowing she was waiting for me to fall. I wanted to show her I didn't need to come to her, and God made it happen by allowing my income tax return to show up in my account and the move was still on. I made the move on the 9th of March instead, and to show additional blessings I was able to have a credit which went towards the next month's rent. BUT GOD!!!!

God has shown me time and time again that He had me. From staying in my house for three and a half years without paying the mortgage, and never being put out, to making sure none of the utilities were turned off, and if they were; He sent someone to handle it. With all this in the past, I had no choice but to trust Him on this matter as well.

It was a moving day, and TJ was in the process of starting his new life. The move was necessary because I knew I didn't have anyone to help and he was it. I had people lined up, but as always no one was available. The move was the worst ever, but it was done and I was glad it was over. Now it was time to prepare for TJ's graduation and I think I was more excited than he was.

21

WHERE THE JOURNEY ENDS
WITH A NEW BEGINNING

It was now April of 2017 and TJ was all over the place. It was time for him to graduate and he was still trying to make things fall into place. As for me I was trying to figure out how I was going to get my business to the point of making money. In October of 2016 I was informed by a woman, who didn't even know me, I needed to start my own business. It caught me off guard because I was there to discuss the behaviors of a client and I was blessed instead. I was told to start a bakery and the interesting part; my grandmother was born in the town where the news was given so I knew it was time to follow through.

My life was going a mile a minute and I needed to finish the book and get my business going in the right direction, but I needed to put everything on hold since TJ was my top priority. He endured a lot from the passing of Ted and the madness with the Air Force. TJ was excited knowing he was about to commission in the Army and all that went with wanting to be in the military. TJ would say he didn't want to be an adult anymore and I would jokingly say, "You are too far into the relationship to go back."

The countdown was on and I was proud of TJ, and everyone knew how excited I was. I was a proud peacock and would show my feathers at the drop of a dime. I was glad my life was falling into play outside of all I had been through. The thought of knowing my baby turned into a man felt good to say. I would thank God every day for the blessing of TJ. I think back on being told I couldn't have any children and TJ was a w blessing and I was truly grateful from the bottom of my heart.

It was Commission Day and I was more excited than TJ. I now had to share my young man with Uncle Sam. I was excited to think TJ would see the world, and that I could vicariously live through his eyes. And guess what? My mother had no say in stopping it. Both my father and I pinned TJ's ranks on him and that sealed the deal for his future. I love TJ more than anything, but he knows he didn't come before God. I watched him in action the entire day and knew it was fate and God had destined it to be.

We survived Commission Day and now it was graduation day. The day turned out to be crazy, but we made it through as well. TJ got up not knowing where his ID was, and it rained the entire day. A few hours later it was official, TJ walked across the stage and the moment the degree was placed in his hand everything wasn't surreal anymore. He was an alumnus and my journey had ended to allow his new beginning to start.

I had endured a lot in my life, but I understand it was the course for my life. If God was to tell us all that we would go through, we would never take on the assignment. I thank God for every trial, knowing it has shaped the woman I am today. God-willing, I will have more life ahead, but this journey was necessary, not for me, but to prepare TJ for what's ahead, and so that his journey wouldn't discourage him. Life itself is never about us, but how others could benefit from our mistakes.

My prayer is that my journey has shown that no matter the obstacles, God has a path cleared and you have to be willing to have your steps ordered, NO MATTER WHAT!

Be Blessed & Enjoy!!!

www.ingramcontent.com/pod-product-compliance
Lightning Source LLC
Chambersburg PA
CBHW071758120626
46550CB00002B/840